TOTALLY CHAOTIC HISTORY
ANCIENT EGYPT GETS UNRULY!

First published 2024 by Walker Books Ltd
87 Vauxhall Walk, London SE11 5HJ

2 4 6 8 10 9 7 5 3 1

Text © 2024 Greg Jenner
Illustrations © 2024 Rikin Parekh

The right of Greg Jenner and Rikin Parekh to be identified as author
and illustrator respectively of this work has been asserted in accordance
with the Copyright, Designs and Patents Act 1988

This book has been typeset in Adobe Garamond Pro

Printed by CPI Group (UK) Ltd, Croydon, CR0 4YY

British Library Cataloguing in Publication Data: a catalogue record for this
book is available from the British Library

ISBN 978-1-4063-9565-5

www.walker.co.uk

MIX
Paper | Supporting
responsible forestry
FSC® C171272

TOTALLY CHAOTIC HISTORY

ANCIENT EGYPT GETS UNRULY!

GREG JENNER

with Dr CAMPBELL PRICE

illustrated by RIKIN PAREKH

WALKER
BOOKS

To Esmé, for bringing the best kind of chaos!
G.J.

For Benjamin, Maria and Noelle
C.P.

WELCOME TO ANCIENT EGYPT!

I guess you picked up this book because you like the sound of ancient Egypt? Maybe you want to know how to build a pyramid or make a mummy, or you'd like to meet some Egyptian gods and goddesses. Well, you're in luck – that's all in this book! But this isn't going to be a dull account of boring dates and dusty old names. Nope! Because this book is really about …

TOTAL CHAOS!!!

(… and also ancient Egypt)

Hello! I'm Greg. I'm a public historian, and my job is to convince you that history is thrilling! To do that, I'm going to take you on a rollicking, roller coaster race through the ENTIRE story of ancient Egypt, from its earliest beginnings to its collapse with Cleopatra. It'll be a wild ride, so maybe bring snacks. (I love snacks!)

As we're zooming along, keep an eye out for my trusty chaos meter. It will tell you whether we're in a period of calm, or if we're heading for TOTAL CHAOS!

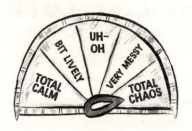

Oh, and we won't be on this journey alone. There are lots of myths about ancient Egypt, so we'll need an expert to figure out what is most likely to have happened! Experts who study ancient Egypt are called Egyptologists, and I know the perfect one to help us. Please meet my super clever co-author, Dr Campbell Price, who is in charge of the Egyptology collections at Manchester Museum.

That's me!

BEEEEEEEP!

If Campbell presses his accuracy alarm, it might be because previous "facts" have since been proven dodgy, or a rival theory may have been suggested. In fact, a group of historians is called an argumentation – we love to disagree!

I'll also scribble in the margins when we get to my fave bits!

WHAT HAPPENS NEXT?!

So, are you ready to get totally chaotic? Events in ancient Egypt may seem neat and obvious when we look back now, but no one living through them had any idea what was going to happen next! Ancient Egyptians didn't know when armies were about to invade, or powerful pharaohs were about to drop dead, or even if giant robot spiders were about to attack with space lasers. (OK, fine, maybe that last one didn't happen!)

Ancient Egyptians couldn't predict that their amazing civilization would last for 3,000 years, just like I have no idea who the prime minister will be in five years' time, or if my favourite football team will ever win a trophy again (I'm still waiting after sixteen miserable years!). And these Egyptians certainly wouldn't have called themselves ancient – they felt like MODERN Egyptians!

So hold on tight, because in this book we're going to imagine we're among the Egyptians, and experience every twist and turn of the ancient world with them!

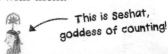
This is Seshat, goddess of counting!

SO YOU THINK YOU KNOW ANCIENT EGYPT?

Right, let's start with a question – what do you think of when I say ancient Egypt? Maybe you're imagining this…

Hey, you know what? None of that is wrong! But the story of ancient Egypt is waaaaaaaaay messier than just mummies, masks, monuments, pyramids, pharaohs and papyrus. It is the story of millions of people, over 3,000 years.

And even though the stuff in the picture is super famous to us now, did you know that…

- Pyramids were only built in the first half of ancient Egyptian history, then they were totally replaced by underground tombs!
- We have millions of papyrus documents, but most of these were written right at the end of ancient Egyptian history!
- Mummification happened throughout, but HOW it was done changed over time!
- Not all Egyptian pharaohs were from Egypt!

Chaotic, right? Basically we've got loads to smash through, and after we're done, you'll never see ancient Egypt in the same way again. Before we get started, let's take a look at a timeline of some of the ancient Egyptian highlights we'll be exploring, and just a few of the hundreds of pharaohs. You'll see it's divided up into the official time periods Egyptologists like Campbell use, and starts over 6,300 years ago…

There were at least 170, belonging to 30 groups called DYNASTIES!

PREDYNASTIC ERA

(c.4300–3000 BCE)

In the Nile valley in north-east Africa, three rival kingdoms scrap for power. The writing system of hieroglyphs is developed.

EARLY DYNASTIC

(c.3000–2686 BCE)

King Narmer becomes the first pharaoh of all Egypt, starting the 1st dynasty. Thinis is the first capital city (it is now lost!), but it's quickly replaced by Narmer's new city called Memphis.

NEW KINGDOM

(c.1550–1069 BCE)

A golden age of famous and powerful pharaohs. They include Hatshepsut (18th dynasty), Akhenaten (18th dynasty), who tries to introduce a new religion with only one god, Tutankhamun (18th dynasty), who is buried in a borrowed tomb, Ramesses the Great (19th dynasty) and Ramesses III (20th dynasty), who gets murdered!

THIRD INTERMEDIATE PERIOD

(c.1069–664 BCE)

EVEN MORE political chaos!!! Assyria violently conquers Egypt, destroying major cities and capturing members of the royal family.

LATE PERIOD

(664–332 BCE)

Egypt faces more invasions. Greek historian Herodotus writes about Egypt – he misunderstands lots of things, but he's still an important source.

MACEDONIAN PERIOD

(332–305 BCE)

A new conqueror arrives: Alexander the Great of Macedon (northern Greece) conquers Egypt.

ANCIENT EGYPT

OLD KINGDOM

(c.2686–2161 BCE)

Here come the pyramids! The Step Pyramid is built by Imhotep (possibly) for Pharaoh Djoser (3rd dynasty). The Great Pyramid of Giza is built for Pharaoh Khufu (4th dynasty). The Great Sphinx of Giza is built for Pharaoh Khafre (4th dynasty).

FIRST INTERMEDIATE PERIOD

(c.2161–2055 BCE)

Everything goes wrong! The pharaohs no longer rule over all of Egypt, and people starve because the crops don't grow. We should probably call this THE DISASTER YEARS!

SECOND INTERMEDIATE PERIOD

(c.1650–1550 BCE)

More chaos with a weirdly boring name! The Hyksos people (from the Middle East) conquer Egypt. But the Hyksos pharaohs later lose power.

MIDDLE KINGDOM

(c.2055–1650 BCE)

Everything calms down a bit. Pyramids are built by workers kept in the town of Hetep-Senwosret. Spells known as the "Book of the Dead" are first written on coffins.

PTOLEMAIC DYNASTY

(305–30 BCE)

Macedonian general Ptolemy becomes the first of the Ptolemaic rulers of Egypt. But this is the final dynasty: when Cleopatra VII dies she is the last of all the pharaohs ever!

ROMAN

(30 BCE–395 CE)

Egypt becomes a part of the Roman Empire.

It all looks pretty straightforward in a neat timeline, right? Unfortunately the reality is a teensy bit more messy! So, if you're ready, let's jump head first into the Nile, and soak up some Egyptian history!

Ancient Egyptians thought of time as both a set of cycles and as one super-long bendy snake stretching eternally into the future!

SPLASH!

Where it all began: Predynastic Egypt – meaning before the pharaohs.

BIT LIVELY
UH-OH
TOTAL CALM
VERY MESSY
TOTAL CHAOS

2
THE NILE IS THE PLACE TO BE

YOU ARE HERE

5000 BCE   4000 BCE   3000 BCE   2000 BCE   1000 BCE   30 BCE

Let's start right back at the beginning, 7,000 years ago, in a time before the pharaohs, the pyramids and everything else recognizably Egyptian. We're in a fertile land in North Africa, with heavy summer rains (called monsoons) filling up the lakes and providing fresh water for drinking wells. People here have learned to farm crops, build villages and keep animals for food and milk. At a place called Nabta Playa, they have built the oldest stone circle in the world (much older than Stonehenge!) and they worship and sacrifice sacred bulls. It's all going rather well.

But then **DISASTER STRIKES!**

The rains stop falling, and the land quickly dries out. Imagine a vast, hot, dry desert – its golden sands warm beneath your feet, and the heat shimmering off the reddish earth. There is no water anywhere; whatever you plant fails to grow and your cows are thirsty and exhausted. Oh, and watch out for stinging scorpions! Now imagine trying to live in this desert – it's tricky, right? So what does everyone do?

Some people become wandering nomads, living in the Arabian and Western deserts, but others head off in search of new lands to settle. Eventually they bump into their salvation. Or rather they TUMBLE head first into it, because they've found a MASSIVE river: the Nile. And it's this discovery that leads to the start of Egypt as we know it!

A VERY BIG RIVER

How massive are we talking, here? Well, the Nile is possibly the longest river on the planet! Annoyingly, some modern scientists are trying to ruin my fun by saying the Amazon (in South America) is slightly longer, but I don't care… I mean, **DOES THIS LOOK LIKE A BOOK ABOUT AQUATIC MEASURING TECHNIQUES TO YOU??!!**

Anyway, the Nile is an astonishing 6,648 kilometres in length and snakes its way through the centre of Egypt, and then fans out into a wide delta where it meets the sea. The Nile actually draws water from two separate branches: the Blue Nile and the White Nile. Oh, and other smaller tributaries, and… **AARGH! WE'RE DOING RIVER SCIENCE AGAIN!**

Greek historian Herodotus said the only reason Egypt could exist was thanks to the "gift of the Nile".

Quick, let's look at a map! See how all the ancient cities hover so close to the Nile's banks, but then you get nothing for thousands of miles either side? That's because of the dark fertile soil there that's very useful – not to mention how handy the river is for transport.

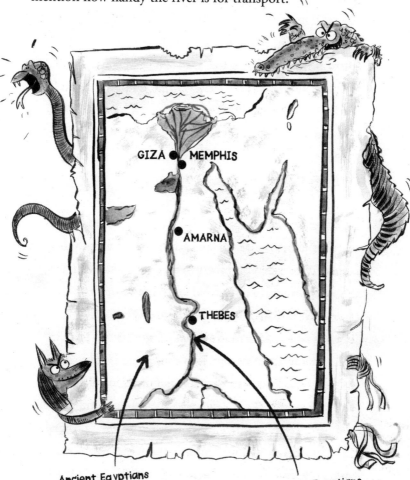

GIZA • • MEMPHIS

•AMARNA

•THEBES

Ancient Egyptians called these barren deserts Deshret ("the Red Land").

Ancient Egyptians called this Kemet ("the Black Land").

NILE = LIFE

Of course, you can't farm crops in the middle of a river, can you? Where would you plant stuff – crammed into hippo bums? Balanced on crocodile backs? Yeah, good luck with that! No, you need soil for plants to grow. And those wandering Egyptians who settle along the river discover the Nile's yearly gift is to swell up, thanks to super-heavy rains in the highlands of Ethiopia (6,500 kilometres away!), so that – from July until October, every year – the Nile gushes out onto the nearby farmland, leaving behind the rich soil of Kemet.

This means ancient Egyptians don't keep four seasons of spring, summer, autumn and winter like we do. They divide their calendar into three seasons of four months: akhet (flood), peret (growing) and shemu (harvest).

Because this yearly flood keeps everyone alive, the Nile itself is sacred. Now, the Egyptians worship lots of gods and goddesses (don't worry, we'll get to them soon!), and anyone who drowns in the Nile or is chomped by a Nile crocodile gets an extra special mummification and becomes a mini god. But mainly it's the yearly flood that is worshipped through the god Hapy. Let's meet them!

NO PLANTS HERE!

FACT FILE: HAPY

Hapy is a blue-skinned figure with a long wig and nice beard, who is often shown offering drinks and food. Hapy is also drawn with a round belly, so is thought to maybe be a pregnant god who combines male and female elements to create new life. Hapy is usually depicted with a papyrus plant on their head, with crocs and frogs hanging out near by. I guess water gods need watery pals! ∎

So for maximum happiness Egyptians need maximum Hapy! This god's sacred floodwaters bring life … but not every year. The Nile can bring chaos! If the water level is too low, not enough land is fertilized, and you get **STARVATION AND FAMINE!** But if the flood levels go too high, then the water doesn't drain away fast enough and the crops don't grow, and then you get **STARVATION AND FAMINE!**

Yes, water is a matter of life and death – yikes! You can see why ancient Egyptian priests obsessively measure the river's height, using little marks on the walls called nilometers (a bit like when grown-ups stand you against a wall and draw a pencil mark to see how much you've grown!).

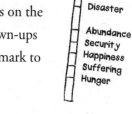

Disaster

Abundance
Security
Happiness
Suffering
Hunger

ROW YOUR BOAT

The Nile isn't just helpful for farming. If you want to get anywhere as a civilization, you need to be able to GET places – that means using the river to travel. The Nile is like a huge blue highway connecting the country. Egyptians don't use wheeled vehicles as much as other ancient societies; they're more into boats! Boats for fishing, boats for transporting stuff, boats for leisure… Even in death, rich Egyptians have model boats in their tombs or boat pictures on the walls. It's fascina—

In art, boats shown with their sails up are travelling south and boats with oars are going north!

OH NO, I TOTALLY FORGOT! We've got to get to the first pharaoh next, but that's 2,000 years away! How do I squeeze all that history into only half a page?! AARGH! DON'T PANIC, GREG!

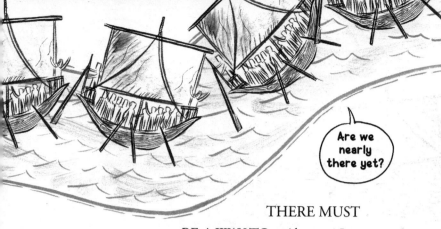

Are we nearly there yet?

THERE MUST BE A WAY TO... Aha, yes! I just found a handy fast-forward button over here! I'll pop it on 10x speed to get us to the next bit...

You'll never fit it all in, Greg!

FAST-FORWARD BUTTON

When people settle on the banks of the Nile, 7,000 years ago, there are no kings! It's just small villages, which grow into towns, and people learn new crafts (pottery, carpentry, beer-brewing, metal-working), and they build bigger buildings for worship, and the rich get richer and more powerful, until you end up with local rulers in charge of cities, and they convince their people to make weapons, and go and conquer nearby cities, so you get lots of small kingdoms, and they fight each other, and eventually you end up with three big kingdoms tussling it out (we think maybe they're called the Tjeni, Nubt and Nekhen), and eventually the Tjeni triumph, and their king becomes the first ever pharaoh of all Egypt. Oh, and his name is Narmer. Done!

Phew, I think we got away with it – onwards! It's time to meet our first pharaoh!

Don't believe everything this guy says!

TOTAL CALM · BIT LIVELY · UH-OH · VERY MESSY · TOTAL CHAOS

3
NARMER DRAMA!

YOU ARE HERE

5000 BCE 4000 BCE 3000 BCE 2000 BCE 1000 BCE 30 BCE

Thanks to zooming at 10x speed, we've reached the first Egyptian pharaoh, around 3000 BCE. Pharaohs are the men (and occasionally women) who rule Egypt. Narmer becomes the first one after his kingdom triumphs over his rivals. Narmer's capital city, Thinis, is located in the bottom half of Egypt – confusingly, this area is called Upper Egypt. His enemies, meanwhile, are in the top bit of Egypt, which is called Lower Egypt. (Sorry, it's all to do with ground height rather than where it is on a map!)

The word pharaoh comes from the term "great house", meaning the palace the king lived in.

Which brings us to one of the most important objects in all of ancient Egyptian history. What do you

22

think it is? Tutankhamun's golden mask? The beautiful bust of Nefertiti? The Rosetta Stone that unlocked how to read hieroglyphs? Nope! They're all very famous, but this one's so special it has never been allowed to leave Egypt. Behold...

What – you've never heard of it?! Oh, all right, let me explain…

Egyptian palettes could have been used for mixing up minerals to turn into make-up, or even as drums for bonging on. But this supersized one is an artwork. And the reason it's so important is because it's such an early example of Egyptian art style and tells us a fascinating story, apparently celebrating Narmer's victory over Lower Egypt.

It's an impressively boastful artwork. I like to imagine this is how it was made…

NARMER'S DEMANDS

Front of the palette

* Most importantly, you need to show ME! (Totally HUGE compared with everyone else, 'cause I'm the best and you're all little dweebs). And I want to be wearing my tall white crown of Upper Egypt.

* Put something to show how I conquered the wet, reedy marshland of Lower Egypt. Maybe some reeds, and then ... uh ... give them a human head or something. I DON'T CARE IF IT'S WEIRD – JUST DO IT!

* Make sure my servant is holding my sandals so I don't get blood on them.

Back of the palette

* I want a big strong bull, because I'm a big strong bull!

* Howszabout ... some long necked-monsters being tamed with ropes?

* A parade of priests and servants – again, I'm HUGE, they're puny!

* Don't forget to stick me in my new red crown of Lower Egypt to show I totally conquered that land!

Got that? Good. GO DO IT!

It sounds weird, but this really is what the Narmer palette shows! It's decorated on both sides, and we can spot Narmer because he's got the special chin beard that all pharaohs wear. On the first side, there's LOADS OF DEAD BODIES, and Narmer smashing his enemy with a club. Narmer is actually shown here as the falcon god Horus (we'll find out more about gods in the next chapter!), and he's got the reedy-headed marshy thing that represents Lower Egypt on a leash, like it's a dog and he's its master. No one ever said ancient Egyptian art was subtle!

When you flip the palette, there's more art showing off how big and strong Narmer is. That means more dead bodies – this time headless. Yuck!

Narmer's name means "Fiercely Attacking Catfish"!

BEEEEEEEEP! • BEEEEEEEP!

ACCURACY ALARM

THE MAN, THE MYTH OR THE LEGEND?

Hang on, Greg – this isn't like an ancient photograph! We don't know if anything shown on the Narmer palette actually happened, or who created it and when! Narmer is said to have united Upper and Lower Egypt into one country, but Egyptologists have spent over 125 years arguing about whether the Narmer palette shows historical truth, a mythical story or a mixture of both! Modern archaeological evidence suggests there wasn't a sudden victory, but instead unification happened slowly. In fact, in some ancient documents, Narmer isn't mentioned at all! Instead we hear of a conqueror called Menes, and one called Hor-Aha. Were they related to Narmer? Different names for him? Was he even real? We don't know for sure!

OK, Campbell's right – the Narmer palette is an amazing object, but it might be too good to be true! But if it isn't true, why would anyone design the palette this way? Maybe to make later pharaohs look all-powerful, so that everyone did what they told them! Loads of things in this book are mysterious and debatable (all part of the fun!). But we do know some things for sure, such as how ancient Egyptians love to worship many, many gods...

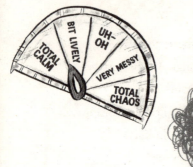

4

ODD GODS

My favourite is Thoth!

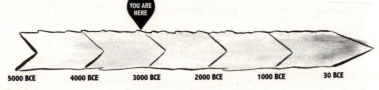

5000 BCE   4000 BCE   3000 BCE   2000 BCE   1000 BCE   30 BCE

Before we move any further forward on our ancient
Egyptian timeline, we need to meet the cast of gods
and goddesses that are so important to Egyptian life.
Ancient Egyptians are super religious, and worship
LOTS of gods and goddesses: this is called polytheism. In
fact, Egyptians see magic and the divine (the fancy word
for godly power) existing almost everywhere. For starters,
the ruling pharaoh is virtually a living god, and gets
100% godified when they die. Egyptians also include

The correct word is "deified"!

natural stuff on the list too. Obviously not everything
is considered holy – there's no divine underpants, for
example. But if the pharaoh wore those pants and got a
hole in them? Well, maybe then they'd be a little bit *holey*
and a little bit *holy*!

Gods are mega-important throughout ancient Egyptian history, but their images change. In the early days, gods were shown wrapped in shrouds with long headdresses. But by now, all the gods are shown standing side-on – or in "profile" (except for Bes, who faces forward). Also, the gods' supernatural powers, jobs, family, enemies and origin stories keep changing. In fact, making sense of the Egyptian gods is like trying to keep up with the messy plot lines of the superhero universe: you've got your good guys, bad guys, feuds, alliances and big action scenes! Yep, it's chaos!

Let's meet some of the most important gods. The key thing to know is that all of them have gold skin, blue hair and bones made of silver or iron. But, oddly, not all of them have human heads...

Made of lapiz lazuli gemstones.

EGYPTIAN GODS

OSIRIS

Ex-human pharaoh murdered by his jealous brother Seth, who chopped him into pieces and scattered them around. Luckily his wife, Isis, stuck him back together! Osiris is god of the underworld, resurrection, the Nile and farming. Dad to Horus.

ISIS

Loyal wife of Osiris who magically restored him to life. Helps Osiris with his underworld duties. Mum to Horus. Not very popular in early Egyptian history, but very famous by the end!

SETH

God of chaos, violence and deserts. Tried to kill his human brother, Osiris, but Seth is not a human. Egyptologists aren't sure what he's meant to be – I reckon he looks like an evil anteater!

HORUS

God of the sky, and protector of pharaohs. Weirdly he has a falcon's head, even though mum and dad are humans! Loses an eye getting vengeance on Seth, but regrows it thanks to Isis and Thoth's magic.

HATHOR

Goddess of partying, fun, fertility, motherhood, welcoming the dead into the afterlife, and war (quite a strange mix!). Often shown as a cow or a cow-headed woman, but sometimes as a tree, a lion or a cobra. Make your mind up, Hathor!

THOTH

God of writing and wisdom, inventor of hieroglyphs, and fixer of Horus's eye! He's either got the head of a long-beaked ibis bird or he's a baboon!

TAWARET

Goddess of pregnancy, childbirth and motherhood. She looks like a hippo with lion's claws and a crocodile tail – don't mess with her or she will mess you up!

RA

God of the sun, bringer of life, sometimes king of all the other gods. Another falcon-headed dude, and Sekhmet's dad. Every day Ra sails through the sky on his boat, moving the sun, and then fights the giant snake Apophis – talk about a difficult commute! Later on in Egyptian history, Ra gets fused with another god called Amun to become Amun-Ra!

BEST OF THE REST

SEKHMET

Terrifying lion-headed goddess who destroys anyone who angers her dad, Ra. Egyptians believe the only way to stop Sekhmet killing everyone is to pour red beer on the fields so she'll mistake it for blood, get drunk and fall asleep!

PTAH

God of craftspeople, sculptors and people who make stuff. Seems like a nice chap, but he's married to the terrifying Sekhmet – how did that happen?!

SOBEK

God of the Nile, and defender of the phar-aohs. With the head of a crocodile, he is a vicious fighter and eats women who cheat on their husbands (but never husbands who cheat on their wives – how unfair!). Later gets smushed together with Ra to become Sobek-Ra, meaning he is promoted to being a sun god!

HAPY

God of the annual Nile flood and farming. A bearded human with a pregnant belly.

ANUBIS

God of mummification. A jackal-headed man who starts out as the god of the dead, but later ends up being demoted to Osiris' mummifying assistant.

KHEPRI

Junior sun god. Has the head of a scarab beetle, because they roll balls of poo along the ground and – apparently – this is like Ra pushing the sun across the sky! Honestly, the poor guy fights a giant snake every day, and his thanks is being compared to a dung beetle?!

BES

God of protecting the home, mums and children. A human dwarf, he loves to party, and he's also great at killing snakes.

BASTET

Cat-headed goddess of motherhood and hunting. Can be ferocious if you anger her!

See, I told you! And that's just *some* of the gods! I know what you're thinking – that's a lot of gods to worship, and some of them seem to have the same jobs. So do Egyptians worship them all in the same way?

Well, the gods who protect homes and families, known as house gods, are more popular with ordinary people, who worship them in a number of ways. They offer them prayers, do magic spells and wear special clothing or jewellery decorated with their images (such as amulets of the Eye of Horus).

Different towns and regions had local favourites too.

Meanwhile the chief gods, like Horus, Osiris, Isis and Ra, are more favoured by the pharaohs. They have temples dedicated to them which are not open to ordinary people. A cult image (a little statue) of the god is kept in the innermost part of the temple – a sort of sacred cupboard – and is only taken out at certain times to clean, clothe, feed and entertain the god. The image is so holy, it's kept behind a curtain to protect people's eyes! Occasionally these statues are taken on trips on a model boat, to visit other gods!

Well, now we know about gods – what's next?

Avert your eyes!

The Old Kingdom period is known as the Age of the Pyramids!

5

PYRAMID SCHEME

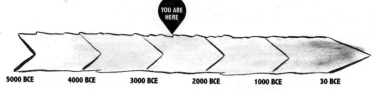

YOU ARE HERE

5000 BCE   4000 BCE   3000 BCE   2000 BCE   1000 BCE   30 BCE

Sorry to rush you, but we've got so much to get through, so let's whizz past the next … uh … like, sixteen pharaohs? You're not missing much; it's basically a variety of rich dudes in big hats! Besides, we need to get to the period known as the Old Kingdom, so that we can reach perhaps the most famous Egyptian thing of all … the pyramids!

The ancient Egyptian word for a pyramid was Mer.

Admittedly, that's 500 years of jumping ahead, and sure, if we did this with modern British royalty, that would be like bouncing from King Henry VIII to Queen Elizabeth II, but you know what? My book, my rules! Let's hit the skip button!

PRESS HERE!
[if nothing happens, turn the page]

Hooray, WE'VE REACHED THE TIME OF THE PYRAMIDS! This is when Egyptians start to build pyramids as burial places for pharaohs (until now, they've been using burial chambers under mastaba tombs).

Later pharaohs were buried in rock tombs in the Valley of the Kings.

The pyramids are also where pharaohs can be worshipped as gods when they die. Imagine planning your own funeral when you're young and healthy, and hiring 10,000 people to make it happen! Inside the pyramids are various chambers, only one of which is for the king's body. There are often smaller pyramids built next door for the queen, as well as nearby temples full of priests (to ensure the worship continues for ever!).

We don't know what the other chambers were for!

And don't they look gorgeous in all their shiny, pointy bigness? Oh, sorry, were you expecting them to be sandy-coloured? No! They're encased in a gleaming outer layer of polished white stone, and possibly a golden pinnacle at the top. This isn't the crumbling ancient relic you've seen on TV; this is brand-new technology! You'll notice that they're built on the edge of the desert, but near enough to water and farmland for people to see them, so these are designed to impress.

But I'll let you in on a little secret: even the most impressive pyramids often start out as a panicky experiment. Stuff goes wrong and people have to learn from their mistakes. In fact, if pyramid building were a televised competition, it would be TOTALLY CHAOTIC!

Welcome to Pyramid Building: Live! The first pharaohs are building royal tombs for themselves at Abydos, and it looks like they've gone for a nice, simple mastaba design, with sloping walls and a flat roof. Strong start!

2800 BCE

Here comes King Djoser and his genius chief architect, Imhotep, and they're piling up six mastabas on top of each other! My word, it's over 60 metres high. This step pyramid is a real step forward in architectural excellence!

2660 BCE

OK, I'm being silly, there are no pyramid-building competitions! But it's true that the Egyptians are experimenting with different styles at this time. And the Great Pyramid is the biggest of all the 100+ pyramids in Egypt, made with an incredible 2.3 million stone blocks. King Sneferu's first effort is called the Meidum Pyramid, but did it *really* collapse, Campbell?

There are also small ones in Sudan – ancient Nubians invaded Egypt and brought the design home!

ACCURACY ALARM

DODGY BUILDERS

BEEEEEEEP! • BEEEEEEEP!

Actually, it's tricky to know what really happened! Some experts think it fell down during construction, but it might have lasted a thousand years before collapsing. Or maybe it never collapsed at all, and the outer stone was just removed and recycled on another project? Who knows!

Good myth-busting, Campbell – in fact, there are LOADS of myths about the pyramids, from who built them to how they did it. Why don't we pause our dash along the timeline and fire some questions at Campbell to test the myths against the facts?

MYTH BUSTER: PYRAMID SPECIAL!

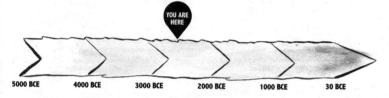

YOU ARE HERE

5000 BCE   4000 BCE   3000 BCE   2000 BCE   1000 BCE   30 BCE

MYTH BUSTER 1

THE PYRAMIDS WERE BUILT BY ALIENS FROM OUTER SPACE!

Nonsense! The ancient Egyptians were plenty clever enough to build their own stuff. And we recently found amazing proof that Egyptians did all the hard work themselves. In 2013, an ancient diary was discovered, written by a guy called Merer – such a discovery is the stuff of archaeologists' dreams! Merer was writing around 2570 BCE, when the Great Pyramid was almost finished. He records the quarrying (digging out) and boat transportation of very fine white limestone

from a place called Tura, on the opposite side of the Nile to Giza. This white stone was probably what made the outer casing of the Great Pyramid shine so dazzlingly bright. Boats also carried massive blocks of granite, used for the internal chambers, from Aswan (a whopping 850 kilometres to the south!). So, no aliens were involved!

THE PYRAMIDS WERE BUILT BY ENSLAVED PEOPLE

This is a tricky one! In the holy books of the Bible, Quran and Torah, the Egyptian pharaoh is the big baddie, and a cruel slave-driver. This made many people assume that the pyramids were built by enslaved people. However, this story was first recorded 2,000 years AFTER the Great Pyramid was built... so it's mostly wrong, but not totally!

We do suspect people from the Middle East and Nubia - such as prisoners of war, and those sold into slavery to pay debts - were forced to work on building projects, and perhaps Egyptian criminals were too. They could be made to live in special towns that were a bit like huge prisons (I suggest you visit the town of Hetep-Senwosret later in the book!) and they were probably treated very cruelly. But archaeology has also shown that much of the pyramid workforce was free Egyptians recruited in the four months when the Nile was flooded, and they were well treated. So the workers were likely a mix of free and unfree people.

PYRAMID BUILDERS WERE VOLUNTEERS WHO WERE PAID FOR THEIR WORK

Hmm, it's complicated. The first thing to say is ancient Egypt didn't have money! Instead workers received cloth, grain, food and drink. We don't know if people volunteered. Maybe they wanted to help glorify the pharaoh? More likely is that the pharaoh's powerful officials could totally boss people around. Just as young men were called up to fight for their country in World War II, ancient Egyptians were possibly called up for national construction duty. This system is called corvée labour – it means you don't get much choice, but you are treated well and allowed to go back to your life afterwards.

Many workers were housed in huge barracks (which archaeologists have found) and given lots of meat and beer. It was definitely hard, dangerous work - but we know one work team called themselves "the drunkards of Khufu", suggesting they had some fun too! If people got hurt, doctors cared for them. And when workers died, some were buried in a cemetery close to the sacred site – probably quite an honour.

PHARAOHS DESIGNED AND BUILT THEIR OWN PYRAMIDS

Seems unlikely! The famous Imhotep took credit for building King Djoser's Step Pyramid, and later became so respected he was turned into a god! But we don't know if he actually designed it himself, or if he just paid the bills. Pyramid building was an enormously complicated project requiring loads of different skills. As well as architects, there were people probably doing similar roles to modern jobs: surveyors, mathematicians, project planners, engineers, carpenters, recruiting sergeants, boat builders, sailors, site foremen, barracks supervisors, doctors and dentists, canteen cooks, beer brewers, cowhands, butchers, laundry teams... so many jobs, and it's very unlikely the pharaoh did any of them!

MYTH BUSTER 5

THERE'S NO WAY ANYONE COULD BUILD THE PYRAMIDS WITH-OUT MODERN TOOLS

It is amazing, isn't it, that the Great Pyramid has 2.3 million super heavy stone blocks, and yet there were no modern power tools to shunt or shape them! But simple tools are all they needed. Egyptians likely had wooden levers and sledges for moving the blocks, copper chisels and flint-tipped hand drills for splitting and shaping them, ramps for raising them up, and mortar to glue them down. We're talking about thousands of people working together for many years, so teamwork made the dream work!

PYRAMIDS COULD TAKE 100 YEARS TO BUILD, AND PHARAOHS COULD DIE BEFORE THEY WERE FINISHED!

We don't know exactly how long it took to build a pyramid, but it's more likely 5 to 30 years, depending on its size. Pyramid construction probably had intensely busy seasons, with 10,000 people all working hard in the months while the Nile was flooded, but then these workers went home to farm their crops. It's possible some pharaohs died before their pyramid was finished, but plenty didn't.

PYRAMIDS WERE FULL OF BOOBY TRAPS TO KILL TOMB ROBBERS!

Sadly, no! That's pure Hollywood fantasy – there are no arrows shooting out of walls, axes swinging down, hissing snakes wriggling on the floor, or huge rolling boulders. We've only found magical curses on the doorways of non-royal tombs. Pyramids often had blocked-up passages to confuse or stop intruders, but nothing lethal!

MYTH BUSTER 8

ER... ACTUALLY, I'VE RUN OUT. TELL ME ABOUT THE GREAT SPHINX INSTEAD!

That's cheating – the Great Sphinx is only NEAR a pyramid! There are many ancient sphinxes, but Giza's famous one was carved from a single block of limestone on the orders of King Khufu's son, Khafre. Sphinx is a later ancient Greek word meaning "strangler", but ancient Egyptians used different names, like Horus in the Horizon. It's 20 metres tall, 73 metres long, and shows the king's head on a lion's body. It marked out a sacred place near the Great Pyramid, and was originally painted in bright colours, but desert winds gradually buried the sphinx beneath the sand. However, one day, a young prince apparently had a snooze in its shadow, and dreamed that the sphinx was asking him to remove the sand! So, his men got digging, and then he cheekily added his name to a slab placed in front of the monument when he became Pharaoh Thutmose IV. If this story is true, it means ancient Egyptians were doing Egyptian archaeology 3,000 years before I was!

Thanks, Campbell – we're now packed full of pyramid knowledge! Let's get moving on our timeline again. I guess from this point onwards it all starts to settle down, as we're leaving the Old Kingdom and heading smoothly into the era that Egyptologists call the First Intermediate Period. That sounds incredibly boring, to be honest. I'm not expecting any drama— WHOA, WHAT'S HAPPENING TO MY CHAOS METER?! I'M SCARED!

FAMINE, FLOODS, FIGHTS AND FAILURE!

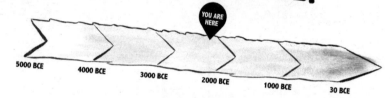

YOU ARE HERE

5000 BCE 4000 BCE 3000 BCE 2000 BCE 1000 BCE 30 BCE

Something is very, very badly wrong – crikey, even the page numbers have gone topsy-turvy, look! The First Intermediate Period is the *dullest* name ever, but suddenly it's chaos everywhere! We've just had mighty pharaohs building huge pyramids, but now we're in 2160 BCE and we're getting reports of famine and fights breaking out all over Egypt, and the pharaohs are too weak to stop any of it. People are even exaggerating that they might have to eat their own kids to survive. (Don't worry – if anyone tries to nibble your leg, just slam this book shut quickly!)

What's happening?! It seems the pharaohs in the capital city of (Memphis) have lost influence, and now wannabe leaders are popping up all over Egypt – and they're fighting with each other for food, resources and land. They're even hiring archers from nearby Nubia to help them defeat fellow Egyptians in battle, so it's all getting really messy!

The ancient Egyptian name is Inebu-hedj.

WHAT'S GOING ON?!

But what's causing all this chaos? Not sure! The Nile has stopped flooding properly, so not enough food is being grown, BUT this drying up started ages ago, in King Khufu's time – it's not a new problem! So maybe something else has kicked off this chaos?

Some scientists think it might have been climate change.

All I can tell you is that the last pharaoh of the Old Kingdom, Pepi II, ruled from the age of six ... until he was ONE HUNDRED YEARS OLD! Perhaps 94 years of one guy being in charge means everything sort of just ... uh ... broke?

WHOOPS!

ART UPDATE!

Talking of things being broken, there's lots of art from this period, but it might not look quite how you expect. You see, these busybody local rulers want to pretend that they're mini pharaohs, so they're hiring local artists to bash out regal portraits. Unfortunately these local artists are poorly-trained compared with the fancy ones in Memphis, so the art looks pretty dodgy!

So we've got fights, famine and total art fails. No wonder this book is going all wonky – this First Intermediate Period is too chaotic to cope with!

IT CAN'T ALL BE BAD

ACCURACY ALARM

I'll admit, things sound bad, but we can't be sure if people who were living through it thought it was a time of crisis! Sure, there was war and hunger – those are scary, and nobody knew how long they would last for – but the reality of this time was pretty up and down. Modern historians only call this a time of crisis because much later Egyptians did, when they looked back at their own history. But obviously people couldn't just hide in a cupboard and wait for stuff to calm down. They still had to farm the land, spend time with their families, look after their animals and pray to the gods. Maybe they were too busy trying to survive to even realize it was a time of crisis? Or maybe there was nothing they could do about it, so why bother complaining?!

Hmm, well, it feels pretty chaotic to me, but the good news is that it seems to be calming down. A guy called Mentuhotep II, from the southern city of Thebes, has overcome all the other rival leaders and is reconquering the whole country. He's very impressive, actually – the crisis has lasted 125 years, and he's been at war for 40 of them, but now he's reclaiming the pharaonic throne, building himself a huge tomb and covering it with glorious art. I think we're entering a new era of ancient Egyptian history – here we go!

The ancient Egyptian name is Waset.

THE MIDDLE KINGDOM!

Phew! So we're now in the year 2055 BCE and… Wait a second – this is called the Middle Kingdom? We're still 500 years away from the midway point in ancient Egyptian history! I mean, no offence, Campbell, but you Egyptologists are USELESS at naming things!

Don't blame me!

All right, well, let's hope the Middle Kingdom is long and peaceful, and nothing like a cranky toddler singing their favourite Disney song by starting too soon, getting lost, and suddenly ending with shouting and screaming!

Oh, and that reminds me… It's not just toddlers who want their mummies. By this point, ancient Egyptians have been mummifying their dead for over a thousand years, but, in the Middle Kingdom, they're really getting the hang of it! Shall we find out more?

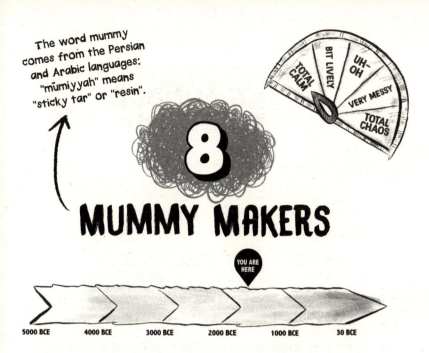

The word mummy comes from the Persian and Arabic languages: "mūmiyyah" means "sticky tar" or "resin".

TOTAL CALM · BIT LIVELY · UH-OH · VERY MESSY · TOTAL CHAOS

8

MUMMY MAKERS

YOU ARE HERE

5000 BCE · 4000 BCE · 3000 BCE · 2000 BCE · 1000 BCE · 30 BCE

I bet you've heard of Egyptian mummies, right? They're super famous, and you can see them in many museums. They're often treated like spooky Halloween costumes – but let's remember that these are the remains of actual people. It's OK to be curious and to study them, but we should be respectful too.

So how do ancient Egyptians make their mummies? Let's pay a visit to an embalming tent and find out for ourselves…

WARNING! This bit involves cutting into a dead body – if that makes you feel upset or queasy, skip ahead to the next section.

MUMMY-MAKING: A HOW TO GUIDE

YOU WILL NEED:

Step 1: Is your client very rich and powerful? Go to step 2 for the FULL PACKAGE – it will take 70 days!

 If poor, go to the BUDGET OPTION

Step 2: Take your long metal hook and slide it into the person's skull through their nostrils. You will need to punch a hole in the top of their nose bone to get into the skull. Now use your tool to scoop out bits of brain, and turn the rest into mushy liquid. Finished? OK, tip the person on their front and pour the rest of the liquid brain out of their nose.

Step 3: Fill the empty skull with resin or linen.

Step 4: Take your sharp knife (be careful!) and slice across the left side of the tummy. Now yank out their lungs, liver, guts and stomach. Don't drop them: these are important! Leave the heart where it is – it will be needed for the person's judgement to get into the afterlife.

Step 5: Put each of the four removed organs in their own canopic jar. These are special jars used during mummification, each representing a different god – like a divine boy band made up of a human (Imsety), a baboon (Hapi), a jackal (Duamutef) and a falcon (Qebehsenuef).

Step 6: Stuff the empty chest with linen, sawdust or whatever you have near by.

Step 7: Cover the body in natron salt and dry it out for around 40 days.

Step 8: Cover the body in sweet-smelling oils.

Step 9: Wrap the body in linen bandages, and maybe write some magic spells on them as protection from scary monsters guarding the journey to the afterlife.

Oh, and maybe slip in a couple of magical amulets (special jewellery).

Step 10: Place the body inside a beautiful wooden coffin. Here, in the Middle Kingdom, there's a brand-new invention: a face mask decorated to make the dead person appear perfectly godlike, with no acne or scars (it's basically an ancient photo filter!). They're now ready to go into their specially carved underground chamber.

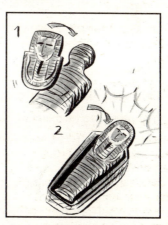

► **BUDGET OPTION**

Of course, there are millions of ordinary Egyptians who can't afford this special treatment, and they don't have luxury tombs waiting for them either. The most afford-able embalming option is to wash the body, wrap it in linen and bury it on the edge of the desert.

JOURNEY TO THE AFTERLIFE!

Why do Egyptians go to all this trouble to mummify someone once they are dead? Well, they believe it helps a person reach the afterlife, where they will live for ever. But getting there isn't easy!

In the Middle Kingdom, a new must-have for the wealthy is lots of hieroglyphic writing on their coffins. These magical texts used to be reserved only for pharaohs, but now rich people have them too. These "Coffin Texts" are filled with over 100 magical spells, prayers and advice to help someone reach the afterlife. Egyptians hope their spirit (the *ba* or *akh*) will leave their mummified body and travel through the scary underworld, sneaking past monsters, a hungry snake and lakes of fire – all the while hoping not to be made to eat loads of smelly poo – until they meet the god Osiris and his jackal-headed assistant Anubis.

Later known as the "Book of the Dead".

They believe Anubis weighs a person's heart against the sacred feather of truth (called *Maat*) to see if they were a good person in life. If the heart weighs the same, Osiris welcomes the dead person into the afterlife – hooray! But if they were mean and selfish, Anubis snatches the heavy heart from the scales and feeds it to the terrifying goddess Ammit (she's part crocodile, part lion, part hippo!), who devours the person's soul, so they vanish for ever.

So all that complicated mummification to preserve the body is pointless if you end up getting munched by Ammit the Devourer!

ACCURACY ALARM

NEW THEORY ALERT

BEEEEEEEP! · BEEEEEEP! ·

I don't think they were PRESERVING their bodies... I think they were TRANSFORMING them!

WHOA WHOA WHOA! All my life I've been told mummification is about preservation – is that wrong? I think we need to have a proper historian debate! Cue the moody studio lighting and banging theme tune, because it's time for...

HISTORIAN HEAD-TO-HEAD

**Two historians,
two different theories:
who will be the winner?
Let's get ready to rumble!**

GREG   CAMPBELL

ROUND 1
WHY DID THEY MAKE MUMMIES?

I put it to you, Dr Campbell, that Egyptologists have found thousands of mummified people because Egyptians wanted to be PRESERVED. They needed their bodies in the afterlife, so they had to ensure they didn't rot away.

Greg, you've got it all wrong – they weren't preserving bodies; they were TRANSFORMING them ... into gods! Lots of mummy masks and coffins (stone ones are called sarcophagi) show the dead person's face with a curly beard, decorated in gold and blue. Remember, the gods have gold skin and blue hair – so I think people were trying to BECOME an Egyptian god and live blissfully in the afterlife.

But why did priests stuff the vital organs into canopic jars? It's because they wanted to preserve them so they'd last for ever!

We only assume canopic jars stored organs. Some of the jars are solid, so you couldn't put anything in them. And it was only the incredibly rich who had their organs removed. Millions of ordinary Egyptians got oil squirted up their bums instead to dissolve their intestines!

ROUND 2
WHAT DOES THE EVIDENCE TELL US?

All right, Campbell, how do you explain this: archaeologists have found lots of precious objects and clothes in rich people's tombs. This is obviously evidence of people packing so they can use these items in the afterlife!

Sure, maybe – but they thought they'd be using this stuff as gods! And don't forget, most Egyptians weren't getting buried like this. Some coffins were used over and over, with a gap where someone's name would be written then wiped off. I'd say they were just speedy transformation-into-gods machines!

OK, but you can't deny that mummification changed over time. Some of the early efforts were really dodgy, and mummies' arms fell off, because priests were still learning how to do it! But later priests changed their brain-scooping technique to reduce damage to the face. Obviously they cared about the body looking correct, therefore IT'S ALL ABOUT PRESERVATION!

Be careful not to assume that earlier priests were clumsy fools! Maybe they wanted bodies to look that way, only for fashions to change? There were also big variations in different regions – not all Egyptians did mummification the same way! So this is NOT PROOF that they were trying to preserve the bodies!

AND THE WINNER IS...

NO ONE

They both had such good arguments!

Oops, sorry about that! Part of the fun of doing history is that there isn't always a right answer. We can only make clever guesses based on the evidence we find. We may never know the truth about mummification, but debating different theories is really important to what historians do, and it's exciting to challenge ourselves with fresh ideas.

One thing you might have noticed with mummification is that there's a big difference in how the rich and poor are treated. This is also true elsewhere in ancient Egypt. Let's visit a new Egyptian town to find out what it is like to be an ordinary Egyptian in the Middle Kingdom…

9
HARD TIMES AT HETEP-SENWOSRET

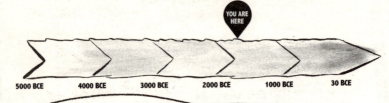

YOU ARE HERE

5000 BCE   4000 BCE   3000 BCE   2000 BCE   1000 BCE   30 BCE

It's 1750 BCE and we're in Hetep-Senwosret, south of the capital city Memphis. This town was originally built for people working on a nearby pyramid, but those workers are long gone and now the town is ready for new people to move in. Would you like to be one of them? Be warned: although there are some lovely houses for wealthy priests and merchants on the east side of town, most of the homes are for poorer folk, and they're not so fancy. Check out this brutally honest estate agent's ad for a poor Egyptian's house, then make up your mind…

Nowadays we call it El-Lahun!

WELCOME TO HETEP-SENWOSRET!

Hi! Tired of busy city life? Bored of working on your farm? Want to hang out near a dead pharaoh? Then why not move to Hetep-Senwosret!

Hetep-Senwosret is BACK! Come and live in our modern Egyptian town, where you'll be part of a close-knit community ... because way too many people are squished together in hot, sweaty houses. You might ask: "Are there lovely green parks and open spaces?" And the answer, obviously, is NO! In the poor part of town there's just hundreds and hundreds of near-identical mud-brick rectangles, and a handful of temples, hemmed in by six-metre-high walls that stop you seeing the rich people's lovely hilltop mansions. And beyond the outer walls is mostly desolate desert, so you can't go anywhere. Sounds perfect, right?

YOUR DREAM HOUSE

Let's take a look at your dream house. It's not-at-all-generously proportioned with four tiny rooms — wow, lucky you! And who needs a bathroom when you can use an old potty a mere two metres away from where your loved ones are eating dinner? Such luxury! As for the bedroom ... there isn't one! Only rich people get that, so why not sleep on the floor, or take advantage of our fantastic flat-roof design and sleep on top of your house in the summer: it's all the fun of camping, but higher up!

TOP-OF-THE-RANGE FACILITIES

What about cooking and lighting? Great question! You can cook all your food on the central hearth. There's no chimney to let the smoke out, so you can enjoy both your dinner and that stinging sensation of the smoke in your eyes and lungs. Delightful! And why not go further with oil lamps and incense burners? They're perfect for illuminating your family gaming sessions — everyone loves to play the board game Senet, or a boisterous round of catch. Just be sure not to accidentally knock a lamp over and set fire to all your stuff. Oops!

LIVING AND LEARNING

Kids, worried about where you can do your homework or wash your school uniform? Don't worry, you can't do either! Only rich boys get an education. You'll do whatever job your parent does, as soon as you're old enough to swing a bucket. As for laundry, you and your mum can scrub your simple linen tunic in the Nile. Watch out for crocodiles: they do love a bitey cuddle!

CREATURE FEATURES

Oh, speaking of which, do you like animals? You're in luck! Here at Hetep-Senwosret you can enjoy noisy, smelly donkeys getting in the way and pooing on the floor. We also offer feral rats and deadly snakes

free of charge in every home. Of course, if — for whatever weird reason — you don't want dangerous vermin in your house, try our handy range of traps, rat-catching cats and dogs, or magical objects dedicated to the household protection gods Tawaret (the hippo goddess who protects children and mothers) and Bes (who loves fighting snakes, ghosts and demons ... and maybe ghost snakes, I dunno?). Yes, we've even got papier-mâché face masks made to look like Bes himself, to help you ward off those lovely lethal spirits!

> So if you need a new home, come to Hetep-Senwosret: where the fun never starts!

INCLUDED

So, do you want to live here? Didn't think so! Sadly, many poor Egyptians have no choice, and it's the same in lots of other towns in ancient Egypt.

Some Egyptologists think the high walls kept them locked in, almost like a prison.

Among the poorest inhabitants of Hetep-Senwosret are probably foreign prisoners of war (from Nubia and West Asia), criminals and people forced to work by officials – their lives are especially tough.

We have lots of papyrus documents that list harsh rules and severe punishments to keep people under control in the town.

Life here is hard for adults, and really dangerous for kids. Disease is rife, food is poor, children are put to work from an early age and dangerous animals are wandering around. Some children die from these illnesses and their bodies are buried under their houses. But, even though things are tough, people still play ball games and board games, and build big communities of friends and neighbours to help them through the hard times.

Still, I don't fancy staying here much longer. And I guess, if it's really bad, people will eventually abandon this town...

Excuse me – where's the exit, please?

THE MYSTERIES OF HETEP-SENWOSRET

You're right that this town eventually emptied out, Greg - but it's a mystery why! In fact, the town was abandoned twice. The pyramid builders left once the pyramid was finished - but we don't know why people came back. And why was it then abandoned for a second time? Us Egyptologists find Hetep-Senwosret a bit of a head-scratcher: so many mysteries we just can't solve!

So there you have it: life is very different for the rich and poor in ancient Egypt. It's not palaces and pyramids for everyone. Now let's get back to our timeline and—WAIT, what's that sound?! Is that … horses' hooves thundering towards us? Do they even have horses in ancient Egypt?! What's happening? Please don't tell me this is ANOTHER stupidly named intermediate period? Even the chaos meter has given up trying to make sense of things!

Yep, and I have no idea what's happening at this point!

10

HELLO, HYKSOS! HELLO, HORSES!

YOU ARE HERE

5000 BCE | 4000 BCE | 3000 BCE | 2000 BCE | 1000 BCE | 30 BCE

Oof! After spending so long looking at the life and death of rich and poor ancient Egyptians, we've stumbled right into the Second Intermediate Period, in 1650 BCE. And it's another time of crisis! The pharaohs in Memphis are looking weak again and different groups are jostling for power. And now we've got a new, foreign pharaoh on the throne – and he's brought horses! So, who is this foreign pharaoh?

FACT FILE:
SOME RANDOM GUY

Annoyingly, we don't know his name! But he is from a group of people called the Heka Khasut (meaning "rulers of foreign lands") who have been immigrating into north-eastern Egypt from the Middle East. We often call them Hyksos (a later ancient Greek word).

The Hyksos set up a power base in the northern city of Avaris – which does lots of trade with cities in the Eastern Mediterranean – and then, at some point, the Hyksos royals somehow gain control of wider Egypt, becoming the 15th dynasty.

People who spoke a different language and had different customs often made their home in ancient Egypt.

Right, so we have the Hyksos and their mysterious pharaoh invading with huge horsey armies, and—

MAKING FRIENDS, NOT WAR?

ACCURACY ALARM

Actually, Greg, we don't know that! Much later Egyptian writings say the Hyksos were violent, terrible invaders, but much later Egyptians were often pretty mean about foreigners. We haven't found any archaeological evidence of big scary armies or terrible war. But we do see new technology coming into Egypt – metal body armour, powerful bows for shooting arrows further and whizzy war chariots. Oh, and yes, to pull those chariots, they introduced horses to Egypt!

What am I doing here? What's my purpose?

Do all of these new things arrive with the Hyksos? It's possible!

Are they violent invaders? Maybe!

Or are they merchants who have moved to Avaris because it's the trade hub for the Nile Delta? Uh … perhaps!

Sometimes Egyptian pharaohs hire foreign soldiers, so could it be that the Hyksos aren't invaders but defenders of Egypt, who settle here, and then eventually challenge the weak Egyptian pharaoh during the crisis of the Second Intermediate Period? I mean, WHO KNOWS?

Hmm, maybe we should rename this time the "I Dunno, Your Guess Is As Good As Mine Period"?!

SO WHO ARE THE HYKSOS?!

Luckily we do know some things for sure. The Hyksos speak a different language, use different pottery, prefer a different style of art on their walls and have their own religious customs. They particularly enjoy worshipping Seth, the god of chaos, and Baal, the god of storms, so they are obviously big fans of messy drama! When they die, they are buried with donkeys and horses next to their graves, but no amulets of Egyptian gods to protect them in the afterlife. So, although they are becoming Egyptians, they keep their own customs.

Yes, remember that ancient Egyptian society was made up of lots of different people!

Oh, but just as I was getting used to the Hyksos, they seem to have lost power after only a hundred years! Does this mean things are going to calm down again? Yep, here comes a new era on the horizon, and it's looking pretty fancy…

THE (VERY OLD) NEW KINGDOM

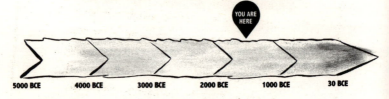

YOU ARE HERE

5000 BCE   4000 BCE   3000 BCE   2000 BCE   1000 BCE   30 BCE

Oh look, we're gliding smoothly into the New Kingdom. This period is also known as the Golden Age, as it's when the Egyptian pharaohs get their power back, and everything has calmed down! Just look at the chaos meter.

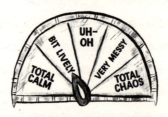

But is it me, or is the New Kingdom YET ANOTHER stupid name? This isn't new, it's happening

3,600 years ago! Can't we just rename all these ancient eras, from newest to oldest? How about Lightly Dusty, Pretty Creaky, Super Old and Mega Ancient?

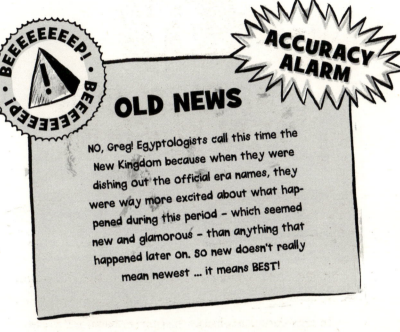

BEEEEEEEP! · BEEEEEEEP!

ACCURACY ALARM

OLD NEWS

NO, Greg! Egyptologists call this time the New Kingdom because when they were dishing out the official era names, they were way more excited about what happened during this period – which seemed new and glamorous – than anything that happened later on. SO new doesn't really mean newest ... it means BEST!

Spoilsport! Fine, so the New Kingdom (meh!) has started in the mid-1500s BCE – give or take a decade – when a king called Ahmose, and his less famous relative Kamose, boot out the Hyksos rulers and unite Egypt under the rule of the 18th dynasty, a new royal family from Thebes. Next, Ahmose's son Amenhotep I takes over as pharaoh, and he's kind of (boring…

→ Not boring! We just don't know very much about his reign.

But then we get Thutmose I, and he's definitely not boring. Just read his fact file!

FACT FILE: THUTMOSE I

Thutmose is a big-time warrior who loves grabbing new lands to pinch goodies for the Egyptian treasury. And he isn't hiding in his palace – he's out there leading the charge. He even claims to have personally killed the king of Nubia in one-on-one combat, and then hung his dead body from the front of his ship as a gruesome trophy. Yuck!

Egyptians also counted their dead enemies after battle by chopping off their hands and piling them up...

Thutmose is probably the first ever pharaoh to build himself a tomb in the famous Valley of the Kings (a stretch of land near Thebes where pharaohs are buried underground), and when he dies his throne goes to his son, Thutmose II.

Unfortunately Thutmose II is a bit rubbish! Thankfully he marries someone impressive. So impressive, in fact, I think she needs her own chapter! Can I get a trumpet fanfare, please?

TOOOOT TOOOOT!

12

HOORAY FOR HATSHEPSUT!

Hatshepsut's name might sound like a sneeze, but in 1450 BCE she's about to become one of the greatest pharaohs of all time – which is even MORE impressive considering she's a woman, and they rarely get to rule Egypt without a man grabbing the throne off them! She isn't the first female pharaoh, and she follows in a line of powerful royal women. But being pharaoh is meant to be a man's job, so Hatshepsut starts appearing in artworks wearing – drum roll – A FALSE BEARD! Smart move, Your Majesty!

However, despite the fake face fuzz, Hatshepsut's route to power is still pretty ... er ... interesting. Let me explain. To ensure power is handed down through the royal dynasty,

Egyptian pharaohs sometimes have to marry members of their own family... So Hatshepsut's mum is her aunt, her dad is her uncle, and as a teenager she marries her half-brother (who is also her cousin!), and he becomes Pharaoh Thutmose II. Must get confusing at family dinners!

Unfortunately Thutmose II is Thut-mostly useless! But he's just dropped dead, and now Hatshepsut is in charge. At first she's only ruling as the caretaker, or regent, on behalf of her stepson/nephew Thutmose III, who is too adorably diddy to rule on his own. But soon she's stepped up to be an official pharaoh, co-ruling with Thut III. And she's got big plans!

Unlike sword-happy Thutmose I, Hatshepsut mostly doesn't want to kill her foreign enemies; instead she wants to trade with them. And this leads to possibly the most famous Egyptian trading trip of all...

HATSHEPSUT'S MEGA-IMPRESSIVE-AND-QUITE-DANGEROUS-SEA-VOYAGE-THAT-TOOK-AGES!

Definitely not its official name!

Just five years after taking the throne (well, borrowing it, maybe?), Hatshepsut dispatches her most trusted sailors on a dangerous voyage to faraway East Africa, to a place

76

called <u>Punt</u>. And it's not exactly popping out to the
corner shop for a loaf of bread and a choccy bar – this is
a very ambitious plan that nobody has tried before. They
must journey 2,000 kilometres to get there, and then
another 2,000 kilometres back… And there are so many
things that could go wrong!

What if there are storms, or pirates, or <u>giant robot</u>
<u>spiders with lasers</u>?! Imagine being Hatshepsut, and
having these doubts bouncing around inside your brain,
with no news of the voyage for months or even years.
And if disaster does strike, a rival could use it as an
excuse to steal your throne, or even murder you!

How many
times, Greg?!
Definitely not
that one...

But look! What's that coming over the horizon? It's
Hatshepsut's ships – what a relief! Shall we see what the
sailors have brought back?

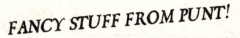

FANCY STUFF FROM PUNT!

- A huge bounty of gold
- Ivory made from hippo and elephant tusks
- Panther skins for making clothes
- Frankincense and myrrh trees for making incense and perfume
- A beautiful type of dark wood called ebony
- Loads of cows
- A gaggle of cheeky monkeys
- Dancers

Hatshepsut is so chuffed by the success, she brags about it in the best place she can think to brag: on the walls of her brand-new, super-fancy, mega-massive mortuary temple, which she orders to be carved into the huge rocky cliffs at Thebes. It's an architectural masterpiece, vibrantly painted in loads of colours, and full of sculptures of Hatshepsut... Wait a sec! Mortuary temples are for dead people! Why is a young, healthy woman with a lovely supply of panther skins planning her funeral?

FUN NOT FUNERAL!

The term "mortuary temple" is an unhelpful clunker we get from past Egyptologists! In fact, these temples were known as "mansions of millions of years", and it was where Hatty expected to be worshipped for ever, with lavish food, drink and entertainment, in the company of her fellow gods (because the pharaoh totally became a full-blown deity after death).

So, Hatshepsut wants to be remembered as a great pharaoh, and builds herself a whopping temple to tell everyone how impressive she is. End of story, right? NO!

Remember, Hatshepsut is only meant to be keeping the throne warm for her underage stepson/nephew Thutmose III. However, when he grows up, she still doesn't give it back! He has to wait for her to die in 1458 BCE. Imagine waiting over twenty years for the throne that is rightfully yours – you'd be proper grumpy, right? Well, many years later, Thutmose suddenly orders all the artworks showing Hatshepsut to be trashed! Yep, he basically pretends she never existed at all – harsh!

NOT-SO-WICKED STEPMOTHER

Not so fast, Greg! Old-fashioned archaeologists said Thutmose III tried to erase all memory of Hatshepsut because she was like a wicked stepmother, but Thutmose might have got on with her just fine. It was probably a question of complicated family trees. The statue smashing happened when Thutmose's son was preparing to rule, and his mother was from a rival family. So maybe Hatshepsut was an awkward reminder of the wrong relations, and they needed her to vanish from memory so no one questioned the claim to the throne?

Cripes! Being an Egyptologist sounds like trying to solve a crime that happened 3,500 years ago… Whatever the truth is, I'm glad Hatshepsut hasn't been erased altogether, as she's deffo my fave. But we haven't got time to hang around with her for ever; there's so much more stuff to cover! What's next on our travels along the timeline?

13
LET'S GET UP AND ATEN!

YOU ARE HERE

5000 BCE   4000 BCE   3000 BCE   2000 BCE   1000 BCE   30 BCE

You know what? I think the chaos of previous eras is over! Yes, I don't want to jinx it, but the New Kingdom seems to be flying. The Egyptian pharaohs have apparently recovered all their old power and wealth; they're trading with foreigners (nice one, Hatshepsut!), and building huge monuments in Thebes, Memphis and elsewhere.

The most exciting thing to tell you about is the new god in town, who is shooting up the divine power rankings to become perhaps the most important god of all. Actually, he's not a *new* god, he's two *old* ones stuck together! We used to have Amun, and we used to have Ra ... but now we have AMUN-RA! Everywhere you look,

The god Amun was originally known as the "hidden one" and was based at Thebes.

81

Big pointy stone sculptures.

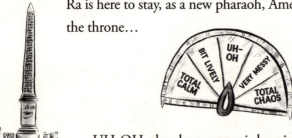

obelisks are being dedicated to him, and the pharaohs are claiming to be his son. I think it's safe to say that Amun-Ra is here to stay, as a new pharaoh, Amenhotep IV, takes the throne…

BIT LIVELY
UH-OH
TOTAL CALM
VERY MESSY
TOTAL CHAOS

UH-OH, the chaos meter is buzzing again! What's happening?

NEWSFLASH!

What the…?

We interrupt this book for an important public announcement from Pharaoh Amenhotep IV!

My fellow Egyptians, for thousands of years, our people have been worshipping the same gods, in the same old ways. It has been part of our culture and our national identity. We have loved and honoured Osiris, Isis, Hathor, Thoth, Horus and now, of course, Amun-Ra. These many gods have been so important to our way of life for so long ...

AND I'M SCRAPPING THE LOT OF THEM!

Yep, what a bunch of rubbish! Me and my lovely wife over here – wave hello, Nefertiti! – much prefer worshipping the Aten, so we've decided you're all going to worship the Aten too! Welcome to the Great Aten Switch-Over!

Now, some of you might be wondering, "What the flipping fudge is the Aten?!" And the simple answer is he's a big, floaty sun disc in the sky, with loads of rays coming out, like arms with hands to give you a friendly tickle ... well, not you, exactly, me! It's me who is important here. Me and my fam, yeah?

So, embrace the change and join me in the great Aten revolution! It's going to be amazing – let's get UP AND ATEN!

Woah, this is huge! Not long after Amenhotep has taken the throne, he's scrapping those famous Egyptian gods for one no one has heard of! And he's even changing his name! Pharaoh Amenhotep IV is now called Akhenaten, in honour of the Aten. And his queen, Nefertiti, is now known as Neferneferuaten.

Meaning "Beautiful are the beauties of Aten, a beautiful woman is here".

This is a lot to get your head around. Luckily Akhenaten has produced this leaflet about the changes...

THE GREAT ATEN SWITCH-OVER

1. **FAITH!** Congrats, you're a monotheist now! That means the Aten is the one and ONLY god. All the other gods? CHUCK THEM IN THE BIN! My soldiers will soon trash their temples and scrub out their names. Particularly Amun-Ra – that guy sucks! Feel free to dispose of old godly objects in your home. You only need the Aten!

2. **CAPITAL CITY!** Exciting news – Egypt's capital city is moving to a brand-new location. It's on the eastern side of the Nile, where the sun rises, and we're calling it Akhetaten ("Horizon of the Aten")! Some of you lowly workers might get called up to come and build it for me – lucky you, eh?

3. **WORSHIP!** We will build new roofless temples to glorify the Aten, and ensure I can always see the sun in the sky. Also, we're putting up tonnes of statues of me, Nefertiti and our lovely daughters, and if he behaves himself and tidies his room, maybe we'll include our son Tutankhaten...

4. **CONSTRUCTION!** We need these new temples and city fast, of course, so I'm happy to say we've invented a new technique for building stuff quickly, using lots of small stone blocks instead of big ones. So expect to be enjoying your brand-new capital city in the next few months.

5. **ART!** We really want this big refresh to have its own look, so Nefertiti and I are thrilled to announce the launch of a beautiful new style of art for Akhetaten. It's time for something hip, modern and forward-thinking. I just know you're all going to love it!

Nefertiti is known for her beauty – there is a famous bust of her in Berlin Museum.

ART UPDATE!

Obviously I made up that press conference, but the facts are true! A few years after taking the throne, Amenhotep IV has ditched the old gods and introduced a weird new style of art that makes the royal family look like space aliens with pointy heads, long arms and pot bellies!

So, do you think this new Aten religion will be popular? Er … nope! Soon after Akhenaten dies, the entire project is scrapped! Akhetaten is abandoned, and the job of restoring the old gods goes to his teenage son, Tutankhaten, who changes his name to Tutankhamun

Its modern name is Amarna.

Wow … at least this is a new type of chaos, right? We've had wars, famines and invasions, but hooray for the novelty factor of a pharaoh with a big, bold idea and way too much time on his hands! Actually, speaking of time, we should pause our timeline and learn how ancient Egyptians tackle that very subject, and everything else to do with science and maths…

Yes, he was THAT Tutankhamun!

14

ASK THOTH!

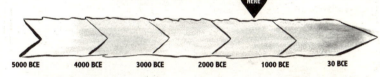

YOU ARE HERE

5000 BCE   4000 BCE   3000 BCE   2000 BCE   1000 BCE   30 BCE

All this amazing architecture keeps getting built all over the place – temples, obelisks, statues, even brand-new cities! – so it's pretty clear that Egyptians know a lot of stuff. I bet when you want to find information, you just look it up online. Well, ancient Egyptians don't have Google – instead they have their god of knowledge and learning, Thoth!

> He's the one who usually has the head of an ibis bird – apart from when he's a baboon!

Can Thoth help us learn about ancient Egyptian science and maths? Let's ask him! (Oh, I forgot, you'll need to offer him a sacrifice in return – busy gods don't do freebies!)

My favourite's duck!

Hey. Thoth! What time is it?

To tell the time you measure the sun's movement with shadow clocks. The sun's shadow is longest in the morning because that's when my buddy, the sun god Ra, rises low in the east. At noon he is directly over you, and then he journeys westwards until sunset. Remember to turn your shadow clock around to face the other direction at noon, or it won't work!

Hey. Thoth! It's dark outside. How do I tell the time at night?

Ask your nearest priest! They watch 36 groups of special stars called decan stars, because a new star rises every hour. Priests also keep complex star charts, allowing them to know when a new week has started. Alternatively, get yourself a water clock – these drain water from one tub into a second, through a small plughole. Use your shadow clock to mark a notch for how high the water reaches each hour, then let it flow at night!

According to my calculations, it's definitely snack time!

Hey, Thoth! How long is an hour?

Depends! A day has 12 hours of daylight and 12 hours of dark. BUT the hours themselves lengthen and shorten depending on the month. In summer, when there is more sunshine, the 12 daylight hours stretch to 75 minutes long! In winter, when it is darker, they are only 45 minutes.

Hey, Thoth! How long is a year?

By studying the sun's movement, priests know a year is exactly 365 and a quarter days long. Don't bother with the quarter (too fiddly!). The three agricultural seasons (flooding, growing, harvest) are each 120 days long, then 5 extra days are added as religious holidays to celebrate us gods (thanks very much!). So, 120 x 3 + 5 = 365! There are 12 months in a year, each 30 days long; and 3 weeks in a month, each 10 days long.

Hey, Thoth! How do I write numbers in hieroglyphs?

Hieroglyphs are the sacred writings I invented (you're welcome!). We Egyptian gods like to count in 1s and 10s and 100s, rather than use 12s and 60s like those weirdo Sumerian gods in Mesopotamia (boooo!). Writing numbers is actually quite easy! Each single digit is one stroke of the pen — so this is how to write **4:** IIII

Now, a **10** is a little hoop, like this: ∩

The symbol for **100** is like a coiled-up rope: ℓ

1,000 looks like a water lily: ⚘

10,000 is a finger: ⫴   **100,000** is a frog: 🐸

To show a massive number like **1,000,000** you draw my excellent colleague, the god Heh, pushing apart two palm leaves:

A palm leaf is the symbol for one year, so by pushing two years apart he's making so much space it's basically *INFINITY*!

OK, let me give you an example of how to write a big number like **3,645:**

Hey, Thoth! How do I measure stuff?

Measures are based on the human body. A royal cubit is the distance from a man's elbow to his fingertips (52.3 cm). We also use shoulder (37.5 cm), big span (26 cm, the distance from a man's stretched-out thumb to his little finger), little span (22.5 cm, from a man's index finger to his little finger), foot (30 cm), fist (11.2 cm), hand (9.4 cm, the width of a man's hand), palm (7.5 cm), and finger (1.85 cm, width not length!).

Hey, Thoth! Can I poke this hippo and then run away?

NO! Never anger a hippo: you WILL die!

Great! Well, now we know about measuring stuff – and when it comes to measuring up in ancient Egyptian history, I'm pretty sure the next pharaoh will say he's the biggest of all!

15

WHAM BAM, RAM (AND FAM)!

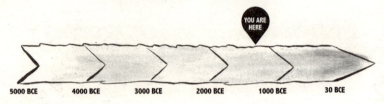

YOU ARE HERE

5000 BCE 4000 BCE 3000 BCE 2000 BCE 1000 BCE 30 BCE

We're still in the glorious golden age of the New Kingdom, and I want to skip past a few pharaohs in order to meet one who is seriously impressive. Hold on to your hats, because here comes King Ramesses the Second (his name rhymes with Hammer-Sneeze the Reckoned)! It's 1279 BCE and he's only 24 years old, and— Crikey, he's already launching a huge war!

He's so great, in fact, he's actually known as Ramesses the Great!

Much like Thutmose I did over 200 years before, Ramesses is battling for land and glory against the mighty Hittite Empire, based to the north-east of Egypt. And after lots of scraps and skirmishes, it's time for them to settle things once and for all with a huge battle!

In the area of what we call Turkey today.

The Egyptians and Hittites get their two armies face to face, at a place called Kadesh, with tens of thousands of soldiers and thousands of war charioteers (good job they've got those horses from the Hyksos to pull them, otherwise they'd be useless!). It's epic, and violent, and nasty, and noisy … but in the end, RAMESSES WINS A MIGHTY EGYPTIAN VICTORY! Sound the heroic trumpets, glory days are here!!!

Wait, why is Campbell's accuracy alarm making that loud honking noise?!

ACCURACY ALARM

BEEEEEEEP! · BEEEEEEEP!

NO WINNERS HERE

Ramesses II was the master of bragging (and it worked, because we now call him Ramesses the Great!), so he proclaimed that he won a mighty victory at Kadesh, and that he personally fought bravely in the middle of the action. He crowed about it in art all over his many temples. One small problem, though: the Hittite king, Muwatallis, also said the same thing! Yep, it was actually a draw, and this is history's first known example of leaders spreading fake news!

Ah, well, that's awkward… With no clear winner, they keep fighting for many more years, until Muwatallis dies and the new Hittite king, Hattusili, offers up a peace treaty and the rival armies go home. With the battles done and dusted, it looks like things are getting a lot more stable on the chaos meter.

Possibly the first ever peace treaty in history!

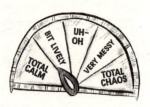

And that means Ramesses now has loads of time for his favourite hobby: building massive monuments dedicated to himself!

RAM'S GRAND DESIGNS

Ramesses builds temples at Thebes and at the capital city of Memphis, and he spends twenty years constructing an enormous temple dedicated to transforming himself into an eternal god after death. Its ancient Egyptian name is "Mansion of millions of years of Usermaatra-setepenra that unites with Thebes-the-city in the domain of Amun"… Imagine having to type that into your satnav!

And if you like the sound of having lots of massive monuments dedicated to you, here is Ramesses' handy guide to construction…

We now call it the Ramesseum!

RAMESSES' CONSTRUCTION TIPS!

TIP 1:
Live longer than other pharaohs! This gives you plenty of time to build more colossal statues than any previous ruler.

TIP 2:
Stick your name on old pharaohs' statues and buildings, or recarve the faces to look more like you … nobody will notice!

TIP 3:
Build a new capital city! And make sure to name it after yourself (mine is Pi-Ramesses, meaning "House of Ramesses")!

TIP 4:
Simplify the artistic style of carving, so statues can be made quicker!

TIP 5:
Don't just erect 50 massive statues of yourself in your new city: sell little models of them too, so the public can keep souvenirs!

Ramesses II sure does love to make big stuff with his face on it. And mini replicas, also with his face on it. But not all of his mini-me replicas are made from stone … some are made from flesh!

That's a really weird way of saying he had kids, Greg!

HAPPY FAMILIES

Yes, Ramesses has lots of wives and girlfriends, and SO MANY kids! How many? Well, think of a number … nope, it's higher than that! He has at least 88 children, but it might be as many as 103!

Between 48 and 50 sons and between 40 and 53 daughters, depending on what ancient sources we read!

Imagine being one of his kids! Your dad is a living god, and you've got 99 step-siblings to deal with … that's a weird family dynamic, isn't it? But one of Ram's children, Khaemwaset, picks up a fascinating hobby…

Which one are you again?

FACT FILE: KHAEMWASET

Khaemwaset is Ramesses' fourth son. He's the high priest in the temple of Ptah in Memphis, where his job includes caring for the sacred Apis bull that Egyptians believe has the power to predict the future. But most interestingly, Khaemwaset spends a lot of time investigating ancient monuments!

Amazingly – much like digging up the Sphinx 150 years earlier – here's another ancient Egyptian prince doing ancient Egyptian archaeology! And he's a little bit like Campbell, actually…

Handsome, funny and clever?

He's a historian, fascinated by statues, pyramids and tombs. It turns out some ancient pharaohs haven't put their names on everything, like Ramesses does, so Khaemwaset rummages around in the archives, and adds the names of those who built the monuments and repairs any damage. Isn't that nice of him!

Oh, right…

However, Khaemwaset also plonks his own name on the stuff he restores, and his dad's name too. So, rather cheekily, Ramesses and Khaemwaset are running around taking credit for Egyptian monuments built centuries before. And sometimes they smash them up and reuse the stone to make new statues of Ramesses instead!

I guess he was an early recycling pioneer too!

LONG-LIVING LEGEND

What with all those massive monuments, and that famous battle he pretended to win, you won't be surprised to hear that Ramesses II becomes an icon for future pharaohs to copy. But what's his secret to success? Not dying, for one thing – he lives until he's 90 years old!

During his 66-year reign, his son Khaemwaset (in his high priest job) has to keep checking Ramesses is still physically fit enough to reign over Egypt. These checks are known as the Heb-Sed jubilee. This sacred ceremony first happens after 30 years of rule, but, from then onwards, Ramesses has to complete it every three years. It's a bit like having an eye test when you're an older driver,

Two more laps, Dad!

except they stick a bull's tail on your bum and make you run laps around the palace to symbolize controlling the boundaries of Upper and Lower Egypt. Most pharaohs are lucky to do it once, but Ramesses lives long enough to do it THIRTEEN times!

Of course, even Ramesses the Great (eventually dies.) The next few pharaohs are a bit disappointing, so it soon becomes fashionable for kings to copy Ramesses' name, perhaps hoping it will make them just as successful. We have Ramesses III – we will get to his story soon! – then it's Ramesses IV, Ramesses V, and then Ramesses VI, and ... urgh, this is taking FOR EVER... Basically you get NINE Ramesses in a row! But none of them match Ramesses II's long-lived legacy.

Ramesses is referred to in some texts simply as "the God", and when he lived to such an old age some people must have thought he would never croak it!

How come Ramesses the Great lived for so long? Maybe he had some excellent medical advice... Let's find out more about that, shall we?

16

FIRST DAY OF MEDICAL SCHOOL

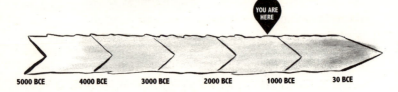

YOU ARE HERE

5000 BCE   4000 BCE   3000 BCE   2000 BCE   1000 BCE   30 BCE

Here in the New Kingdom, Egypt is at its cultural and military height, and it's also a good time for studying medicine. Egyptian doctors are becoming particularly skilled at treating various illnesses, and they're writing lots of their cures down in handy books for others to read.

We have several of these papyrus texts, and they tell us a lot of fascinating detail!

Ancient Egyptian doctors believe the gods give them healing magic, called Heka. Doctors are a bit like priests – in fact, priests devoted to the most fearsome gods, like lioness-headed Sekhmet, are renowned as the best doctors. I guess they need to be ready to undo all the damage when she goes on one of her violent rampages! Doctors find that patients respond best when they wear a god mask to look like either Bes or Horus – because nothing says "Get well soon!" like a face full of falcon beak!

Both men and women can be doctors, and most doctors specialize in one area of the body – they might be a dentist, a limb surgeon, a skin expert, a bonesetter, or someone who removes boils or helps deliver babies. Egyptian doctors divide illnesses into three categories: easily fixable, long-term manageable and sadly incurable. If a disease is treatable, medical papyrus texts have official treatments. Only if the patient is still poorly after a week is a doctor allowed to experiment with new cures.

Do you fancy learning how to treat patients? Great! Let's enrol at Doctor Peseshet's medical school, and hopefully we'll find out why she's carrying that bottle of animal wee?! Yuck!

Welcome, students. I am the pharaoh's royal physician. I am a bottom doctor: I specialize in illnesses to do with eating, digesting and what goes wrong when our bums hurt. My job title is Shepherd of the King's Rear...

STOP LAUGHING, IT'S A VERY PRESTIGIOUS ROLE! There are many hundreds of cures to learn, but here are the easiest to remember...

TOOTHACHE

Honey goes in the mouth to treat toothache. It's also good for coughs. And diarrhoea. And ... loads of things, actually!

I got the honey ... now I need a cure for bee stings!

WOUNDS

Obviously you want to put a juicy slab of uncooked meat on open wounds – it stops the bleeding! Honey can also go directly on wounds, because it's antiseptic.

HEADACHE

This one's easy – get your patient to chew on bark from the willow tree.

BITES

If your patient has been stung by a scorpion or bitten by a snake, write a magical spell on a statue, pour water over it, and then drink the water. You can also rub it on the bite too – very versatile, that one.

TUMMY ACHE

This is my specialism. Tummy ache is caused by a demon in the belly, so draw a magic spell on the belly button, ask the gods for help, and hopefully the patient will fart out the demon in no time! Or you might want to chase out a demon or spirit by fumigating it – this means burning nice-smelling incense, which attracts the gods into your home. You can then politely ask them to get rid of the pesky demon for you.

CHILDBIRTH

Remember, the hippo goddess Tawaret is the protector of mums and kids, so if you are delivering a baby, use her magical tusks to clamp the baby's head when you carefully yank it out!

GENERAL HEALING

A good doctor always carries a pen to scribble healing spells in hieroglyphs directly onto people's tongues, so the cure is absorbed into the body. Or you can write out a spell on a long thin piece of papyrus that measures exactly the same length as the patient, then roll it up and wear it around the neck – easier with kids, but it takes ages with someone as tall as King Ramesses III!

Beer, wine and milk are healthy drinks that can give your patient strength. And you'll need plenty of animal products. Ideally we're talking blood from bats and lizards, lots of urine, the placenta from a cat and the bile from a cow. Oh, and dried-up poo from crocodiles, flies, hippos, sheep, geese, etc. etc. are all super-useful cures – although you might need to mix in some of that beer, wine and milk if you don't want your patient to be sick all over your shoes!

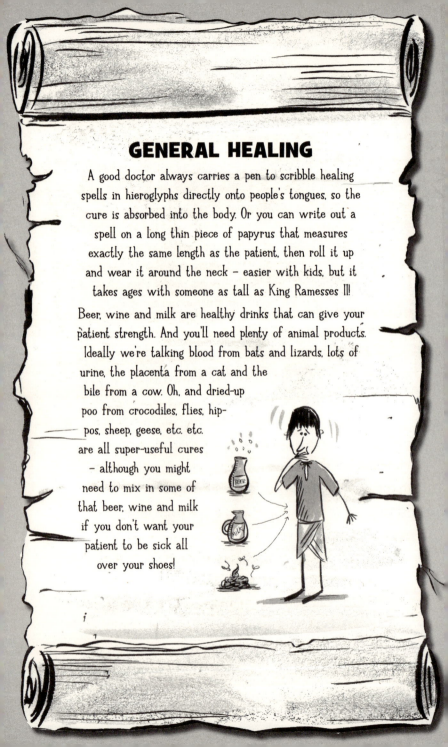

Hmm, best not to try any of those treatments at home. I especially don't like the sound of that croc poo – gross!

ACCURACY ALARM

POO OR NO POO?

To be honest, we're not sure if this was real croc poo, or if that's just the name of a plant! However, some of those cures aren't as bizarre as you might think. For example, chewing on willow bark actually did work for headaches, as it contains similar chemicals to aspirin, a treatment used by modern doctors! Ancient Egyptian doctors might actually have had medical training apprenticeships – they were really smart.

Exactly, Campbell! Ancient Egyptian doctors might not have all the fancy technology found in modern hospitals, but they do seem to have some good solutions to common problems. We know that in the New Kingdom they can repair broken bones with splints and bandages, do minor skin surgeries with knives and scissors, treat patients with all sorts of natural remedies, and ensure people eat a healthy diet.

Ah, well, that was a fascinating lesson ... and a bit gross! But I can hear a lot of noise coming from the nearby palace, and I don't think it's a good noise... We'd better go see what's happening!

17

THERE'S BEEN A MURDER!

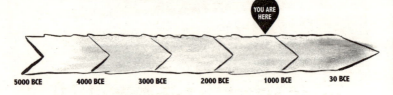

YOU ARE HERE

5000 BCE   4000 BCE   3000 BCE   2000 BCE   1000 BCE   30 BCE

Uh-oh! While we were studying at medicine school, political events have become pretty turbulent again!

Yep, Ramesses II may have been the greatest of all the pharaohs (in his opinion!), but we've had six underwhelming rulers since, and the sudden arrival of ferocious foreigners in the north, dubbed the Sea Peoples, is causing havoc. Now Egypt has a pharaoh who's a total Ramesses wannabe. In fact, he's *also* called Ramesses, and he's named his kids after Ramesses' kids – what a copycat!

This new Ramesses tribute act – Ramesses III – started out as a great military hero, successfully fighting off the Sea Peoples, but long wars are bad for the economy. In fact, 30 years into Ramesses' reign, I'm hearing rumours of droughts and famines, and workers going on strike! This isn't good news. The pharaoh's enemies are lurking everywhere, and he might need to watch out for—

WHOA!!! THE CHAOS METER JUST EXPLODED!!!

HUGE NEWS – THE KING HAS BEEN MURDERED!

Think you can figure out who did it? Fire up your console, because here comes the role-playing game where you hunt...

THE PHARAOH'S ASSASSIN!

Take control of police chief Ahmose and investigate the violent murder of Pharaoh Ramesses III. Try to solve the mystery of who wanted him dead ... bad luck, after 30 years of disappointing rule, there are LOADS of suspects!

LEVEL 1
INTERROGATE THE SUSPECTS

Who has the most to gain from killing the king?

 Suspects #1: The builders of the royal tomb! They went on strike because Ramesses didn't pay them – did another ambitious royal bribe them to get rid of the pharaoh?

 **Suspects #2:** The desert people! They keep attacking Egypt's lands and then scurrying back to their own territory – do they want to take power? Maybe, but good luck arresting them; they're hiding in the scorching hot desert!

 Suspects #3: Foreign prisoners of war! They were branded with red-hot metal stamps and forced by Ramesses III to build his temples – are they seeking revenge?

Suspect #4: The new king! Did Ramesses' eldest son get tired of waiting for his turn to rule? The newly crowned Pharaoh Ramesses IV had much to gain, but he's the one ordering you to solve the crime. Is he innocent, or just pretending to be outraged about his dad's murder?

Suspect #5: An ambitious queen! Did one of the pharaoh's wives betray him so her son could take power? Queen Tiye believed her son Pentaweret should have been first in line for the throne. But watch out: she won't think twice about finishing you off if you insult her honour!

Suspect #6: The king's doctor! He certainly got close to the pharaoh, but the murder weapon was a knife. Wouldn't he use sneaky poison instead, and pretend it was death by natural illness?

Suspect #7: The king's magician! He was seen around the king at the time of his death ... but why would he kill his boss?

Suspects #8: The Sea Peoples! Who are these mysterious invaders? Are they fierce attackers, or refugees? Ramesses III fought them off twenty years ago, and sent some to live in faraway Canaan – is this their way of getting back into Egypt? You might need to send a diplomat to interrogate them, and that could take months!

LEVEL 2
EXAMINE THE BODY

Talk to the embalmers doing the pharaoh's mummification. You can see his throat has been cut with a knife, and his toe has been hacked off with an axe – two weapons suggests it wasn't a lone assassin. Cutting the king's throat is very risky – it guarantees a murder investigation! Was the knife attack a drastic last resort after previous, sneakier attempts had failed?

LEVEL 3
HUNT FOR CLUES

Visit the scene of the crime. The pharaoh died in his palace, so surely no peasants or foreigners would have been allowed past the guards and into his private chambers? The king must have trusted the assassins.

LEVEL 4
SOLVE THE CASE!

Now you've considered the evidence, you must solve the crime. Be careful – whoever you accuse will be horribly executed! But get it wrong, and YOU might be for the chop! So who do you think did it?

CHOOSE WISELY

or it's

GAME OVER!

Did you guess? The murderer is...

ACCURACY ALARM

MANY MURDERERS

BEEEEEEEP! ¡BEEEEEEEP!

Well, it's unlikely she did it herself! The investigation discovered the plot had been led by Queen Tiye, who wanted her son Pentaweret to rule instead of his older half-brother. The plot was called the Harem Conspiracy ("harem" is an Arabic word for the palace where the king's wives and girlfriends lived together). Queen Tiye's accomplices, including the king's doctor and his magician, had tried cursing Ramesses III with magic, but that didn't work. Unfortunately for Queen Tiye, Ramesses IV seized the throne before Pentaweret could grab it, and his inquiry found 38 people were guilty of treason, including Tiye!

Yep, crime doesn't pay! Queen Tiye and the main plotters are brutally executed, but young Pentaweret is forced to kill himself.

A body was found which might be his, without the usual mummification treatment – maybe it was a punishment?

Luckily we have the official court case written on a five-metre-long papyrus scroll, plus the bodies of the victim and his treacherous son, to help us understand this crime!

Phew, that was exciting. But surely things will calm down now in Egyptian history, right? RIGHT?!

18

NEWBIE NUBIANS AND NAUGHTY NEO-ASSYRIANS!

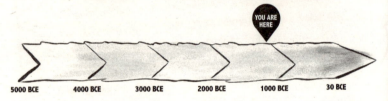

YOU ARE HERE

| 5000 BCE | 4000 BCE | 3000 BCE | 2000 BCE | 1000 BCE | 30 BCE |

OH NO! There's still over 1,000 years of ancient Egyptian history to go, but we're running out of chapters! And if that wasn't bad enough, the last pharaoh of the New Kingdom, Ramesses XI, has just died and in 1069 BCE we're crashing into ANOTHER messy intermediate period. It's time for drastic measures. I'm going to have to hit the fast-forward button to get us through the next few hundred years!

Last one, I promise!

BIG BREATH … HERE WE GO!

FAST-FORWARD BUTTON

Sooooooo, it's the THIRD INTERMEDIATE PERIOD – yeah, you know the story by now! Pharaohs lose power, Egypt splits up, and a new royal family (the 21st dynasty) pop up, but they're only strong enough to rule Lower Egypt (in the north) while the rest of Egypt is run by the high priests of Thebes (in the south). Then in 943 BCE, the 22nd dynasty shows up. They're originally from Libya (west of Egypt) and they cling to power for 200 years, until their cousins – the unoriginally named 23rd dynasty – take over. Suddenly, in 732 BCE, we get a new pharaoh called Tefnakht I and he's only gone and founded the 24th dynasty, hasn't he? And I predict he'll be a great succe— Oh, he's dead! Oh well, here comes his ambitious son, Bakenranef— Whoops, he's been captured by a rival king from the 25th dynasty, called Shebitku. Hang on! How have we got TWO Egyptian dynasties at the same time?! Never mind, Shebitku has just murdered Bakenranef by SETTING HIM ON FIRE – horrifying! That's the end of the short-lived 24th dynasty!

Phew, I feel a bit woozy after that! But we've made it as far as the 25th dynasty, and it's worth pausing to look at their fascinating origins. Have a look at the fact file while I have a lie-down…

FACT FILE:
NUBIAN PHARAOHS

The 25th dynasty are five pharaohs from a kingdom called Kush (or Nubia), which controls land south of Egypt (modern Sudan). In 744 BCE, their ruler, King Piye, conquers all of Egypt. Although the Nubians are invaders, there have been centuries of trade and battles between both countries, so the Nubians already know plenty about Egyptian culture and are happy to keep lots of their religious customs. In fact, the Nubians like Egyptian pyramids so much, they build lots of their own in Sudan!

BRACE FOR MORE CHAOS!

You know how I said it was chaos before? Well, it's about to get EVEN MORE CHAOTIC! It is an intermediate period, after all. Never mind the Nubians; now the super-powerful Neo-Assyrian Empire has arrived with a massive army to invade Egypt!

They ruled the territory to the north-east of Egypt.

Back and forth the fighting goes, over nearly 60 years, until King Ashurbanipal of Assyria smashes through

Egypt in 664 BCE. And that means we can wave bye-bye to the Third Intermediate Period and say hello to…

THE LATE PERIOD

Hey, this isn't a bad name for once!

You're welcome!

Will this new era mean things calm down? Absolutely not! King Ashurbanipal gets locked in more battles for control of Egypt, including his infamous Sack of Thebes. "Sacking" is basically when soldiers run through a city, stealing everything of value – treasure, furniture, palace doors, horses, sculptures, the Egyptian royal family, prisoners, etc.! The Sack of Thebes is a MASSIVE news story, talked about thousands of miles away! It's such mayhem, it's set the chaos meter on fire.

Hang on, it's getting worse: Ashurbanipal is dead, and the entire Neo-Assyrian Empire just collapsed like a castle made of soggy waffles! Now what happens??!! Oh, of course, here comes another superpower – the Neo-Babylonians* – and what do you do when you're a fancy new empire? You declare war on Egypt, of course!

*Also based to the north-east of Egypt.

115

The Babylonian warlord Nebuchadnezzar II
– fun name! – steams into Egypt, but he doesn't
succeed in taking over. Instead we end up
with a brilliant Egyptian soldier called Ahmose
being declared Pharaoh Ahmose II in 570
BCE. Impressive Ahmose reigns for 44 years,
makes Egypt rich and powerful, and goes down
in history as the last great Egyptian pharaoh.
What a relief! I think we can relax…

Unexpectedly, Egyptologists just discovered an earlier ruler called Ahmose, meaning Ahmose I is now Ahmose II, and THIS Ahmose II is now actually Ahmose III... Confusing, sorry!

HERE COME THE PERSIANS!

SORRY, I WAS WRONG! Stop relaxing immediately!

NOT AGAIN?!

Here comes ANOTHER foreign empire – they're called the Persians, and they're about to have a major impact on Egypt!

From Western Asia...

It seems the Persian king, Cambyses, is very angry with Ahmose II. The story goes that he wanted to marry Ahmose's daughter, but Ahmose tried to trick Cambyses by sending him a pretend princess instead. Cambyses is furious and invades Egypt, which gives us the famous…

BATTLE OF PELUSIUM!

Ahmose II actually dies before Cambyses reaches Egypt – but why waste a good march, hey? So Cambyses gathers his soldiers at Pelusium, in the far north of Egypt, in 525 BCE. He has a genius plan: the Persians paint on their shields (and maybe even clutch in their arms) LOADS OF CUTE CATS!!!

What do you mean that doesn't sound like a genius battle plan?! You see, the Persians know that the Egyptians worship miaowing moggies, so won't dare shoot their arrows in case they accidentally hurt a lovely kitty! And that's how Persia wins the battle and Egypt loses its national independence. WHAT A CAT-ASTROPHE!

They're so CUTE!

PERSIANS IN CHARGE

So the Persians have taken control of Egypt. The Egyptians do rebel against Persian rule, and in 404 BCE they get their country back … but then the Persians take over again in 343 BCE!

Phew, that was an intense 600 years! Are you feeling OK? If you got dizzy and passed out, here's a quick recap:

Mighty Egypt collapsed, lost to the Nubians, outlasted the Neo-Assyrians, survived the Neo-Babylonians, were outwitted by an army of Persian cats, bounced back and then lost to the Persians all over again … simple!

We've ended this high-speed history session with the Persians controlling Egypt – and they are really NOT popular. But what IS popular with Egyptians? Cats, of course! I've got the purrrrrfect chapter next…

19
MIAOWING MUMMIES

5000 BCE   4000 BCE   3000 BCE   2000 BCE   1000 BCE   30 BCE

As you saw from the Persians' clever tactics at the Battle of Pelusium, it seems everyone knows how much the Egyptians love cats – in fact, they worship them! They believe that gods can take the form of cats and so they are seen as sacred symbols.

But actually, lots of animals have an important role in ancient Egyptian worship. There are many places in Late Period Egypt where we can see this in action. So, if you're an animal lover, perhaps you'd like to take a sight-seeing tour of these animal-friendly hotspots! May I offer you a brochure…?

VISIT BUBASTIS!

It's a cat lover's paradise in Bubastis, the northern city dedicated to the cat-headed goddess Bastet. There are sacred cats in temples, cat art on the walls, cat jewellery on sale in markets ... and SOOOO MANY DEAD CATS!

This is where cats are brought for mummification and burial. Ancient Egyptians treasure their feline friends so much that when their cat dies, the family shave off their own eyebrows to show they're in mourning! At least, that's what the ancient Greek writer Herodotus claims. So if you see an Egyptian with no eyebrows, they're either mourning a moggy, or they accidentally put their face too close to a candle!

Although ... most of these dead cats are actually being given as offerings to Bastet. Yikes! Maybe alive-animal lovers should visit Saqqara instead?

VISIT SAQQARA!

Next stop on our tour is a little further south, at the charming necropolis of Saqqara!

This is where many pharaohs are buried (including Djoser in his Step Pyramid), but it's also a special place for appreciating lovely animals ... and then wrapping them in bandages and chucking them in the ground! Hmm, maybe "animal-friendly" is the wrong phrase for our brochure?

Saqqara is an ABSOLUTELY HUGE tourist hotspot, but also a famous animal cemetery. Tens of millions of animals are crammed into the special underground tombs called catacombs. To be totally honest, these mummified critters aren't beloved pets who died after a lifetime of cuddles. No, to please the gods, there is a teensy bit of animal sacrifice... (OK, maybe sliiiiightly more than *teensy*, but don't tell anyone I said that!) We're talking dead ibises! Dead baboons! Dead falcons! Maybe even the occasional crocodile! These animals are sacred, but there's also a killing to be made in the animal mummification trade. Oops, sorry about that. But there are definitely some living animals at the next stop on our tour, I promise!

VISIT THE SERAPEUM!

No animal lover's trip to Saqqara is complete without visiting the most important beast in all of Egypt – the Apis bull! This fortune-telling bull has special white markings on its black skin and is so special that it lives in a lavish temple in Memphis, worshipped as a living god by high-ranking priests.

When one dies, a new bull with the same markings has to be found. So do you want to see this divine bull? Well, YOU CAN'T! It's only sacred pilgrims making a religious journey who are allowed to look at it, sorry! But you can see their mummified and bejewelled corpses, if you want? They get buried inside massive 60-tonne sarcophagi in a huge underground catacomb called the Serapeum. King Psamtik I has upgraded these tombs recently, so they are even more impressive to visit!

> **Sign up for our animal tour of Egypt today...**
> **Just don't expect to see many of them alive!**

Hmm, maybe ancient Egyptians aren't such animal lovers after all. In fact, animal mummification has become especially popular here in the Late Period, with many species getting the bandage treatment. Although they don't do spiders – maybe it's just too fiddly with all the legs?! Anyway, it seems ancient Egyptians might not be the best cat-sitters if you want to go on holiday...

ACCURACY ALARM

BEEEEEEEP! · BEEEEEEEP!

GIFTS NOT PETS

You're right, Greg! We should be careful calling Egyptians animal lovers. To them, animals were gifts to the gods, not pets! Interestingly, modern scanning technology tells us that only a third of these mummies contains a full animal; the rest have only part of an animal, or no animal parts at all! Were the Egyptians cheating the gods by giving them fakes? I don't think so! I think a mummy only needed to contain a very small part of a sacred animal for the gods to accept it as a gift. Which brings me back to my argument that mummification wasn't about preservation—

Sorry to interrupt you, Campbell, but a massive army has just shown up, and I don't think they're here for a holiday! Indeed, their leader is the most famous conqueror on the planet right now... TAKE COVER!

20
ALEXANDER THE GREAT

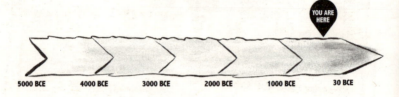

5000 BCE   4000 BCE   3000 BCE   2000 BCE   1000 BCE   30 BCE

Prepare the barricades! Sharpen your weapons! Put on your armour! Because Egypt is about to face the greatest warrior alive, King Alexander of Macedon.

An area in modern-day Greece.

The Persians may have been in power for a while, but it looks like this young warrior is about to shake things up. You might know him better as Alexander the Great. Here's why!

GULP!

This impressive Greek became king of Macedon at just twenty years old. He is terrifyingly brilliant at crushing enemy armies, including the mighty force belonging to King Darius III of Persia at the Battle of Issus. After that victory, Alexander marches on the Persian city of Gaza, which is said to be un-stormable ... but Alexander storms it anyway! Now Alexander is building his own empire, as the Persian Empire topples before him!

Alexander is now 25 years old. He is relentless, he is merciless, and he's heading straight for Persian-controlled Egypt. This is surely going to be a massive fight: let's take ringside seats...

ROYAL RUMBLE

You join us live on pay-per-papyrus-view for the biggest smackdown since Ramesses II pretended to win at Kadesh!

In the red corner stands the challenger: he's young, he's gorgeous, he's ALEXXXXXANNNNDER THE GREAAAAAAAT!!!

And in the blue corner ... they call him THE GOVERNOR, because that's his job! It's MAZACES THE SATRAP!

DING, DING! And it's on!

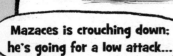

AtG 0 - 0 MtS

Mazaces is crouching down; he's going for a low attack...

OH MY WORD, he's kissing Alexander's feet! MAZACES JUST SURRENDERED WITHOUT THROWING A SINGLE PUNCH! We have a new champion in Memphis – and it's Alexander the Great!

Rather than being a scary invader, Alexander is greeted as a heroic saviour by cheering Egyptian crowds. Yes, after nearly 200 years of meddling with Egypt's religious customs, the Persian overlords are hated by the Egyptian people. Governor Mazaces wisely realizes he won't win a battle and welcomes the new Greek conqueror, allowing Alexander to sweep into Memphis without even raising his sword! And what's the first thing Alexander does? He puts on some Greek athletic games, hosts a music festival, and – best of all – offers a sacrifice to the divine Apis bull, which Egyptians love to worship, and which the Persian rulers weren't big fans of. Smart move! Now everyone thinks Alexander the Great is … uh … pretty great.

A GREAT CITY

Alexander builds his own brand-new city on Egypt's northern coast. He calls it Alexandria, named after himself, because the guy has an ego the size of a planet! He declares himself pharaoh, and heads off west to a place in the desert called Siwa, where he talks to the oracle – a magical priest who can speak for the gods. The oracle tells Alexander that he is the son of the top Greek god, Zeus (who the Egyptians call Amun), which means Alexander can declare himself a living god too – lucky old him, eh?

Alexandria looks out across the Mediterranean sea towards Greece, Alexander's homeland.

Conquer land, tick!
Build new city, tick!
Become a living god, tick!
Egypt? Completed it, mate.

And with that, the newly divine Alexander immediately leaves Egypt to invade somewhere else. You'd think the Egyptians would be annoyed to be dumped by their glam new boyfriend, but they don't seem to mind. In fact, when Alexander returns to Alexandria, after 323 BCE, they don't even shout at him because ... well, he's dead, and that would make for such an awkward funeral!

Alexander was probably buried in Alexandria, but his tomb has never been found. Roman leaders Julius Caesar and Augustus both visited him, though, so he must be around somewhere!

A NEW DYNASTY

So who is ruling Egypt now? Well, when Alexander dies, his Macedonian Empire goes a bit wobbly. A chap called Ptolemy – a military general and one of Alexander's best friends – ends up running Egypt as governor. In 305 BCE, he decides he may as well make himself the pharaoh. This begins the 31st dynasty in Egyptian history...

ACCURACY ALARM

DAFT DYNASTIES

BEEEEEEEP! • BEEEEEEEP!

Sorry, Greg, we don't call it that! Historians stop counting Egyptian dynasties after the 30th! Instead we call it the Ptolemaic dynasty – pronounced TOL-OH-MAY-ICK (the P at the beginning is silent!) – because King Ptolemy's descendants ruled Egypt for 275 years. Confusingly Egyptologists also call this period the Hellenistic era, because ancient Greeks actually called themselves Hellenes (not Greeks!). Tricky, isn't it?

Uh... That is so confusing!!! Honestly, Egyptology is such a weird mess sometimes. But not as messy as the violent family arguments between Egypt's final Ptolemaic rulers. Let's find out more about them – including one INCREDIBLY famous queen!

21

THE TRUE-ISH DIARY OF QUEEN CLEOPATRA VII

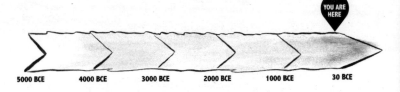

YOU ARE HERE

5000 BCE 4000 BCE 3000 BCE 2000 BCE 1000 BCE 30 BCE

We're nearly at the end of our Egyptian adventure. A final dynasty of Greek rulers has taken control, and although they rule for 275 years, I say let's skip right to one of the most famous queens of all time.

You've probably heard of Cleopatra. She is born in 69 BCE and is the last of the Egyptian pharaohs. And one of the reasons she's so famous is because she's a drama queen with the messiest love life and a ruthless approach to playing happy families! Just imagine if she'd kept a diary…

SEE INSIDE

Age 11: Dear diary, busy day with my tutor – I've decided to learn Egyptian, on top of my other eight languages. My dad (Pharaoh Ptolemy XII) says I don't need to bother: Greek is good enough for him ... and he's a living god! Off hunting now, hope I catch a hippo!

Age 12: DISASTER!!! Dad has annoyed the Egyptians so much that they've chased him out! He's fled to Rome. My big sister Berenike is saying she's the pharaoh now?! I don't know who to side with – I'm scared!

Age 14: Berenike is, like, super-duper DEAD! Dad had a secret deal with the Romans, and they helped him storm back into Alexandria and retake his throne! Poor Berenike was executed for treason. I'm so shook! Dad's told me it's time I learn how to rule by sharing the throne with him. I mean, HELLO! Can't a girl get some time to process stuff first, Dad??!!

That's a chaotic childhood, right? So, Cleopatra co-rules Egypt until her father dies, but as a woman she's not allowed to carry on ruling alone. Instead she shares power with her half-brother Ptolemy XIII, and – even weirder – she has to MARRY him too! He's just a kid, so eighteen-year-old Cleo still has to make all the decisions, and she's— NOPE! Spoke too soon!

Ptolemy shoves Cleo off the throne so he can rule by himself, forcing her to run away to Syria with her little sister Arsinoe, in search of soldiers to support her. But then, powerful Roman politician Julius Caesar suddenly shows up in Egypt! He's furious at Ptolemy for executing Pompey, Caesar's Roman enemy. Apparently only Romans can kill Romans?! Anyway, Cleopatra wants Caesar's support against Ptolemy, but she's stuck in faraway Syria – if only she could get a secret meeting with him…

Age 22: I'm a SNEAKY GENIUS! Caesar was staying in my old palace in Alexandria, so I snuck past the guards by disguising myself as fresh laundry. I make a very convincing duvet! I jumped out, and Caesar totally fancied me, so now we're a couple, or whatevs, even though he's got a wife back home (plus he's 30 years older than me!). And we have a super cute baby. I've called him Ptolemy (like my dad … and brother … and grandad – look, it's tradition, OK!), but I'm nicknaming him Caesarion, which means "Mini Caesar": how totally adorbs!

Age 23: Good news! My annoying teenage brother is dead. Not my fault, honest! He was in a huge sea battle against Caesar, and apparently Ptolemy drowned while trying to swim to safety. That's why we invented boats, you idiot! So I'm queen of Egypt again! Yay! Unfortunately my sis Arsinoe betrayed me to join Ptolemy's team, so I've banished her to a temple, far away in Ephesus. But I didn't kill her, so I'm nicer than my dad. It means I've only got one sibling left, Ptolemy XIV. He's just a little kid, and thankfully I don't have to marry him too – I'm old enough to rule on my own!

Oops, sorry! Egypt isn't prepared to have a woman ruling on her own, so Cleopatra IS forced to marry little Ptolemy XIV and share power again! And things get even worse – over in Rome, Julius Caesar is now so powerful he declares himself dictator for life! It's a bit like being king. Sounds great, right? WRONG! Romans HATE being ruled by kings, so Caesar's former friends murder him! Cleo and Caesarion are visiting Rome when it happens, and they have to flee for their lives! Unlucky Cleo desperately needs a new Roman lover to keep them safe...

Age 28: GREAT NEWS! Found a new Roman protector. Plus he's a total hottie! Mark Antony is a friend of Caesar's, and he's one of the three politicians sharing power in Rome (it's him, Octavian and Marcus Lepidus – they call themselves the Triumvirate). Honestly, this is such a great idea! Plus, did I mention he's very hot?! We played this hilarious game to see who could host the most expensive dinner party – I won by drinking a priceless pearl dissolved in wine! The look on his face was also priceless, ha ha ha!

Age 30: OK, slight hiccup. Mark Antony just married Octavian's sister, Octavia, even though we're in love. So he's now cheating on the sister of his closest ally with a foreign queen. Is that bad? Nah, it'll probably be fine...

I'm starting to think this is not going to end well! Anyway, Cleopatra and Mark Antony have three children together: Cleopatra Selene (it means moon!), Alexander Helios (sun!) and Ptolemy (it's a well-worn family name!). But what about Caesarion? Cleo makes him her co-ruler by killing her current co-ruler and brother/husband (uh ... brusband?!), Ptolemy XIV. And just to make sure she's got rid of all her rivals to the throne, Cleopatra sends an assassin to sister Arsinoe's temple to kill her too! Best of all, she convinces Mark Antony to divorce Octavia and promise that Caesarion will inherit Julius Caesar's old lands. Maybe everything has worked out brilliantly for Cleopatra after all!

Hmm, that's odd, why is the chaos meter going so wild...?

Age 37: So, Octavian just ended the Triumvirate and declared war on me and Mark Antony! Apparently the divorce was an insult to his sister (plus murdering people in temples is considered quite impolite in Rome – who knew?), and Octavian says he is the rightful heir to Julius Caesar's lands, not Caesarion. Oh well! We'll fight off these invading Romans, easy-peasy! Although lots of our sailors and soldiers just switched sides to Octavian's army... Never mind, must dash for a big sea battle at Actium. I'm confident we'll win!

Age 38: WE LOST! RUN AWAY! RUN AWAY!

Age 39: Made it back to Alexandria, but Octavian is coming for us. There's no escape. Mark Antony has decided to end his own life with a sword, and I'm going to take fatal poison. Nobody told me it would be so hard being pharaoh. At least my children have a new home. Amazingly Octavia – who Mark Antony dumped – has agreed to raise our kids as her own. I hope they have long, happy lives (and don't turn on each other, like my brothers and sisters did). Farewell, diary. It's been an adventure. Cleopatra VII x

Sadly Octavian killed Caesarion, but Alexander Helios was probably allowed to live, and his twin sister, Cleopatra Selene, later became a powerful queen in North Africa!

Wowsers! She lived quite a life, that Cleo…

And with her dramatic death also comes the end of Egyptian independence: after 3,000 years, Egypt is now ruled by Rome as a province of its empire. Which means we've reached the end of our chaotic Egyptian timeline! Good job – I think the chaos meter needs new batteries! But before we finish, there's one more mystery to solve: how on earth do we know all this stuff about ancient Egypt anyway? Time to talk archaeology!

22

ROSETTA READERS

Before we can go and slump on the sofa, we need to explore the ENORMOUSLY important archaeological discoveries that happened hundreds and hundreds of years AFTER the time of the ancient Egyptians. Because without these discoveries, we would know so much less about Egypt's history. And Campbell's job would be much harder!

You see, after everything came crashing down after Cleopatra, it wasn't like everyone forgot about the ancient Egyptians. People studied their monuments and art. And from medieval times until the 1800s, some rich Europeans ate little bits of ancient mummified Egyptians to help them recover from illness! Historians call this bizarre cannibalism "corpse medicine", although I prefer to call it *dead-icine* (YUCK)!

However, there were still many mysteries about ancient Egypt, and the biggest mystery was what their hieroglyphs meant. For 1,500 years, no one could read them. Some scholars in the 1600s even argued they weren't words at all, but magical symbols! But no one knew what secrets they might tell us about ancient Egyptian life. So, what happened? How did we crack the code?

Well, it's all thanks to the discovery of the famous Rosetta Stone. I guess you could say the people who first translated it were the original "rock" stars!

Rock on!

THE STORY OF THE ROSETTA STONE

To find out how this huge discovery went down, let's hop to 1798. We're a long way from the time of the pharaohs, and Egypt is now ruled by the Turkish Ottoman Empire.

But wait! French military genius Napoleon Bonaparte has just invaded with a huge army! He's been an ancient history fanboy since childhood, obsessing over stories of Alexander the Great and Julius Caesar. They both conquered Egypt, so he wants a go too! Napoleon has brought with him clever-clogs scholars and fancy-pants artists to help record as much ancient Egyptian archaeology as possible.

There were 167 people in his Nerd Squad, called "savants" (learned scholars) in French!

One day in 1799, French soldiers are digging a new fort, in a place called Rashid (or Rosetta in ancient Greek), and they find a chunky stone slab covered with three types of carved writing. At the top are 14 lines of hieroglyphs – how confusing! Below them are 32 lines of a different, squiggly script – how mysterious! And below them are 54 lines of ancient Greek – how translatable! The local commander, Pierre-François Bouchard, realizes this is an important discovery, so he sends the Rosetta Stone off to his boss.

Merveilleux! Is it a paperweight?

However, the British suddenly join forces with the Ottomans and boot Napoleon out of Egypt! The Brits take all the ancient Egyptian stuff they've found (including the Rosetta Stone) and send it to King George III, who gives it to the British Museum in London. The Egyptians are not given the option of keeping it in their homeland.

OK, but how does this help with the hieroglyphs? Well, it's time to meet two brilliant boffins, who see the Rosetta Stone and realize it's their chance to crack the code! British doctor Thomas Young and the young French scholar Jean-François Champollion spot that the same message (about Pharaoh Ptolemy V) is carved at the bottom of the stone in the three different languages: ancient Greek, the mysterious squiggly script, and hieroglyphs. This is totally thrilling! They can use the ancient Greek text to decode the other two types of writing!

But it isn't easy, and Young and Champollion are both racing to be first. So, how do they tackle the challenge? Well, why don't you have a go yourself! Are you good at solving puzzles? Prepare to have your brain stretched!

DECODING THE ROSETTA STONE

This mega-complicated flow chart shows you just a tiny number of the tricky questions that Young and Champollion have to wrestle with.

Find Ptolemy's name at the very bottom of the Greek text!

↓

Now look for it at the bottom of the hieroglyphs - found it?

↓

Maybe? It's just squiggles, but there is an oval edge around it, as if it's special.

↓

Any other words with oval edges?

↓

Yeah! Maybe they symbolize names? There's lots of names in the Greek text.

↓

But only six words have oval edges in the hieroglyphs. Why?

↓

Maybe only royal names have oval edges?

Errr ... no? ←

↓

Try again! His name must be there somewhere!

Bottom to top, like in Libyco-Berber?

↑

Top to bottom, like in Japanese?

↑

Right to left, like in Hebrew?

↑

Left to right, like in English?

↑

Hang on! In which direction are we reading the text?

Does a squiggle represent an idea?

↑

Does a squiggle represent a sound?

↑

Does a squiggle represent what it looks like?

↑

Wow! But why is Ptolemy written with all those squiggles?

↑

Cool! So if the one at the bottom is a royal name - it must be Ptolemy! You just translated the first ever hieroglyph!!!

Mind-bending, isn't it? Young makes the first break-
through when he notices that some words are surrounded
by oval borders (called <u>cartouches</u>). He realizes that
these hieroglyphs must represent royal names (for
example Ptolemy V). But it'll take another twenty
years to figure out the rest!

A French word for the cartridge that goes on the outside of a bullet.

Young and Champollion have to work out
which direction to read the writing. What if it's one
way on the first line, but backwards, mirror-style, on
the second (this is a weird ancient Greek style called
boustrophedon)? Confusing, isn't it?

There's also no punctuation or spaces between the
words. So, howdoyouknowwhenawordhasendedandanewonehasstarted?!

And there are lots of squiggles that look like birds,
eyes, snakes, plants, etc... What do they mean?!

In 1822, over twenty years after the stone was dug
up, Champollion tells his brother he has cracked the
code, and then nearly dies from exhaustion! Luckily he
survives to share the solution with the world, and everyone is very excited ... apart from Thomas Young, who is
pretty grumpy to have lost the decoding race!

So, what is Champollion's discovery? Let's learn how
to hieroglyph!

HIEROGLYPHS FOR BEGINNERS

Here's a quick guide to the key things you need to know to read hieroglyphs. But be warned – it turns out hieroglyphs are really, REALLY complex!

- Those squiggles represent a MIX of sounds, ideas and pictures of real things.
- There are no vowels, only consonants.
- This means one word can have different meanings!
- To solve this, extra symbols called determinatives are added on the end of a word to give more information. We don't do this in English, but if we did, "right" could have → (direction), or ✓ (correct) or 📜 (a right granted in law).
- Oh, and it gets worse: hieroglyphs can be read right to left, left to right and sometimes top to bottom! Here's three examples, in three directions: they all spell "mummy"!

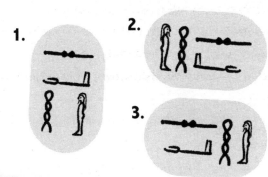

1.

2.

3.

ANOTHER CODE CRACKED!

Oh, and are you wondering about that other mysterious squiggly script on the Rosetta Stone? Well, they cracked that code too! Various scholars – including Young and Champollion – work out that this is demotic, a more everyday script that evolved out of hieroglyphs. So one lump of rock helped to solve two ancient language mysteries!

THE END OF THE STORY...?

Lovely, well, that's hieroglyphs sorted, and... Oh no, wait a second! You see, the Rosetta Stone was carved in 196 BCE, during the final Ptolemaic dynasty (Ptolemy V was Cleopatra's great-great-great-grandad!). But if there's one thing we've learned on our ancient Egyptian adventure, it's that things change massively over these 3,000 years of Egypt's history. What if ancient writing styles had changed over time, and Champollion's decoding formula doesn't work for much older hieroglyphs from the days of Ramesses II, or even Narmer? After all, if you go back a thousand years, medieval English is spelled totally different from modern English!

This could be a DISASTER!

But all is not lost. Champollion discovers an ancient document that lists loads of pharaohs. He compares it with a much older list of kings written on the walls of a temple belonging to Ramesses the Great's dad. Amazingly, the lists look the same! This means hieroglyphs have not changed in 1,000 years, and his translation system will work for ALL OF EGYPTIAN HISTORY – HOORAY!

Even better, it also reveals something that YOU already learned at the start of this book: ancient Egypt is actually waaaaaaay older than the Romans and Greeks! The Egyptian king lists have dates going far beyond the founding of Rome, so historians realize Egypt extends way back beyond this. By decoding hieroglyphs, Egyptologists can now translate stuff written thousands of years ago by the once-mysterious ancient Egyptians. It means Campbell and his colleagues can read names on statues and walls, ingredients in recipe books, medical advice, legal cases, peace treaties, even what people scribbled in their diaries about how to build a pyramid!

My favourite is decoding ancient graffiti!

The Rosetta Stone wasn't just the key to unlocking a lost language. It helped move us so much closer to understanding the ancient Egyptians themselves, and all aspects of their culture. Of course, there are many mysteries still to debate (we historians sure do love to argue!). But without the Rosetta Stone, Campbell would have ended up doing a totally different job, and this book would have been a three-page pamphlet!

TUT'S TOMB
TREASURES

You've seen how a key discovery massively altered our view of this ancient civilization, right? But, believe it or not, there's another Egyptological discovery that is even more famous than the Rosetta Stone. I'm talking about Tutankhamun's tomb!

Remember <u>Tut</u>? He was a pharaoh way back in the New Kingdom period – and to be honest, he wasn't very exciting. But Tutankhamun's mummy mask is probably one of the things you pictured when I asked you to think of ancient Egypt. And the reason he becomes one of the most famous people ever (despite being dead for over 3,000 years) is because the discovery of his treasure-packed tomb in 1922 kick-starts a media sensation called Tutmania!

His dad, Akhenaten, was the one who ditched all the gods and introduced Aten worship!

But there are a lot of dodgy stories about Tut and his tomb. So let's do some myth-busting!

DODGY STORY 1:
Howard Carter
discovered the tomb alone.

The archaeologist credited with finding Tut's tomb is Englishman Howard Carter. He pretends to be properly posh, but is actually an ordinary fella who first goes to Egypt aged just seventeen. Because Egypt is ruled by the British Empire at this time, the job of digging up its ancient history isn't given to an Egyptian – it's given to our mustachioed Mr Carter. He's good at overseeing the work, but he argues with others and loses his job. Instead he starts working for a mega-rich Brit called Lord Carnarvon, who is Egypt-obsessed.

For fifteen years they hunt for an amazing discovery, with no luck. Carnarvon wants to give up the expensive search, but Carter begs for one more try. In early November 1922, one of Carter's team of expert Egyptian diggers finds a mysterious staircase dug deep into the ground in the Valley of the Kings. They cut a hole in the doorway at the bottom, Carter lifts up a candle and peers through, his colleague says: "What can you see?" and Carter reportedly

Often it's said to be a twelve-year-old Egyptian boy called Hussein Abdel-Rassoul, though not all historians agree.

replies: "Wonderful things." He is gazing at thousands of gold objects glistening inside an ancient tomb!

So did Howard Carter find the tomb on his own? NOT REALLY! He needed loads of support, including from many skilled Egyptians, and he didn't even find the staircase himself. But he was the first to enter the tomb, and he was in charge of its exploration. He gets all the glory!

DODGY STORY 2:
Tutankhamun's treasures show he was one of the most important pharaohs of all time.

Tut's tomb contains waaaaaay too many treasures to list. Here are some highlights…

King Tut's iconic golden mummy mask inlaid with coloured glass and semi-precious gemstones (it weighs 10 kg!)

Two daggers: one gold, and one made from an iron meteorite that crashed from outer space!

Model boats

145 spare pairs of underpants (that seems too many, right?!)

Solid gold sandals

Six chariots

Two silver and copper trumpets

Various types of leather and metal armour, including a multicoloured neckpiece with scarab beetle design

Gilded wooden statues of Tutankhamun hunting hippos

Golden diadem (a type of crown)

Beds which sloped downwards and had a footboard to stop Tut sliding off the bottom

Golden belt buckle showing him riding his chariot

King Tutankhamun sure did love gold stuff … but his treasures were really nothing special! All pharaohs were buried with incredible things like this. Unfortunately royal tombs were usually robbed by ancient thieves. However, Tutankhamun died so unexpectedly, aged just nineteen, that his fancy tomb hadn't been cut into the rocky hillside of the Valley of the Kings yet. Instead his body went into a borrowed tomb, much lower in the valley. There was a tiny bit of robbing, but – before the thieves could return for the heavy stuff – there was a flash flood that covered up the tomb entrance with mud. It was a total fluke that it stayed hidden for 3,245 years!

Before his discovery, Tutankhamun was considered only a minor pharaoh, and the only interesting thing about him was that his parents – Akhenaten and Nefertiti – had tried to start their own religion (the Great Aten Switch-Over, remember?). The discovery of his tomb made him super famous, but he was never as powerful as Ramesses the Great or many other important pharaohs.

Hey, not fair! Ramesses ruled for 66 years, I did my best, OK?!

DODGY STORY 3:
Tutankhamun's tomb is cursed!

You heard me – people believe there is a fatal curse linked to the tomb! What's that about?

Well, Lord Carnarvon doesn't want loads of journalists and photographers getting in the way around the tomb, so he agrees a deal with *The Times* newspaper in London so it will exclusively print the photos in January 1923. Later the *Illustrated London News* produces much higher quality pics. Readers are amazed and newspaper sales shoot up!

Over the next few years, the media sensation (nicknamed Tutmania) continues! You can see ancient Egyptian culture in art, pottery, books, hairstyles and women's fashion; biscuit tins and face creams are marketed with Tut's tomb as design inspiration; there are Tut-inspired jazz songs and dance crazes; cinemas and theatres are built to look like Egyptian palaces; and loads of tourists flock to Egypt.

The famous mummy mask of blue and gold wasn't revealed to the public until 1925. Tut never wore it while alive; it would have been way too heavy and hot!

However, with *The Times* and *Illustrated London News* greedily hoarding all the best photos, other newspapers get annoyed at being left out! So they start a cheeky rumour to sell their own papers. Helped by a couple of famous authors, the papers spin a story that the tomb of King Tut is cursed by ancient magic – anyone who disturbs him is doomed!

They claim to have plenty of evidence. Lord Carnarvon dies just two weeks after visiting the tomb, and his pet bird gets eaten by a cobra (the symbol of the ancient pharaohs!). There's also a power cut in Cairo the night that Carnarvon dies. Spooooky! Over the next few years, several other people connected to the dig also die in violent or unusual ways, giving journalists another excuse for a dramatic headline. So do you believe in the curse?

I don't, because it's not spooky at all! Lord Carnarvon is already poorly when he gets bitten by a mosquito and dies of a very common disease. Birds often get eaten by snakes, and power cuts happen all the time in big cities – particularly in 1923, when early electric lights are pretty unreliable!

Another so-called "victim" – the scientist who X-rays King Tut's mummy – is already seriously ill before the dig, and dies after a complicated operation goes wrong. And all those other deaths? They're just weird coincidences and unlucky accidents.

But – here's the crucial thing – the curse is OBVIOUSLY NOT TRUE!!! Why? Because Howard Carter – the first man in the tomb, who even pockets precious objects to keep for himself – DOESN'T die mysteriously. Nope, he lives for another sixteen years!

As historians we have to be careful to follow the facts. Just because it's a good story, doesn't mean it's true!

And what about Hussein Abdel-Rassoul, the young boy who many believe first found the staircase, and who posed for a photo with one of King Tut's golden necklaces? He lives to 100! In fact, loads of the archaeologists and visitors to the tomb enjoy long lives. The curse of King Tut is a bunch of garbage, but it sells a lot of newspapers.

AN EGYPTIAN LEGACY

Phew, that was some good myth-busting! Of course, one thing that IS true is that the discovery of King Tut is huge for Egyptians too! In 1922, they had just gained their partial independence from Britain, so they are understandably grumpy when all the best photos get printed in British newspapers, and the Egyptian public aren't allowed to visit the tomb. Egyptian politicians use Tutmania to fire up a cultural movement called pharaonism that proclaims a brighter future for Egypt by harking back to its ancient glories. It's a reminder that history is often politically useful in the present day.

So, the discovery of King Tutankhamun's tomb is a worldwide phenomenon! And a hundred years later, it's still considered the greatest archaeological discovery ever. Pretty amazing, right? It's part of the reason so many people are interested in ancient Egypt today, including Campbell! *

I could write about the awesomeness of ancient Egypt all day. But I'm afraid we've run out of pages!

* My great-aunt Betty gave me Carter's book when I was a kid – it confirmed my interest in Egyptology!

That was absolutely epic!

CHAOS = COMPLETE!

There's just enough time to sneak in a cheeky farewell before you shut this book... Here goes!

It's been a tonne of fun racing through thousands of years with you – I hope you've caught your breath!

I also hope it's obvious that I wasn't exaggerating when I said history is pure CHAOS! In fact, rather than being a simple story, it's almost like history is a living, breathing creature that wriggles and squirms as we try to catch it! And why is it always moving? Because every new generation asks fresh questions of the past, so it never sits still.

And there's so much history! Campbell and I have given you a crash course in the main bits of ancient Egyptian history, but there are always many other things to discover. You might think that we're historical experts, but we learn new stuff every day!

If your curiosity is suddenly shooting up, and you're potty for pyramids and thirsty for Thoth, why not visit a museum? Or there are loads of other brilliant books and websites to feast upon. Maybe one day, if you're really lucky, you might even visit Egypt! You could bump into Campbell when he's out there translating an ancient statue. Do give him a friendly wave!

For now, it's time for us to say goodbye. But remember, history doesn't stop when you close this book. You're living through it every day. And just like in ancient Egypt, you never know when it's about to get …

TOTALLY CHAOTIC!

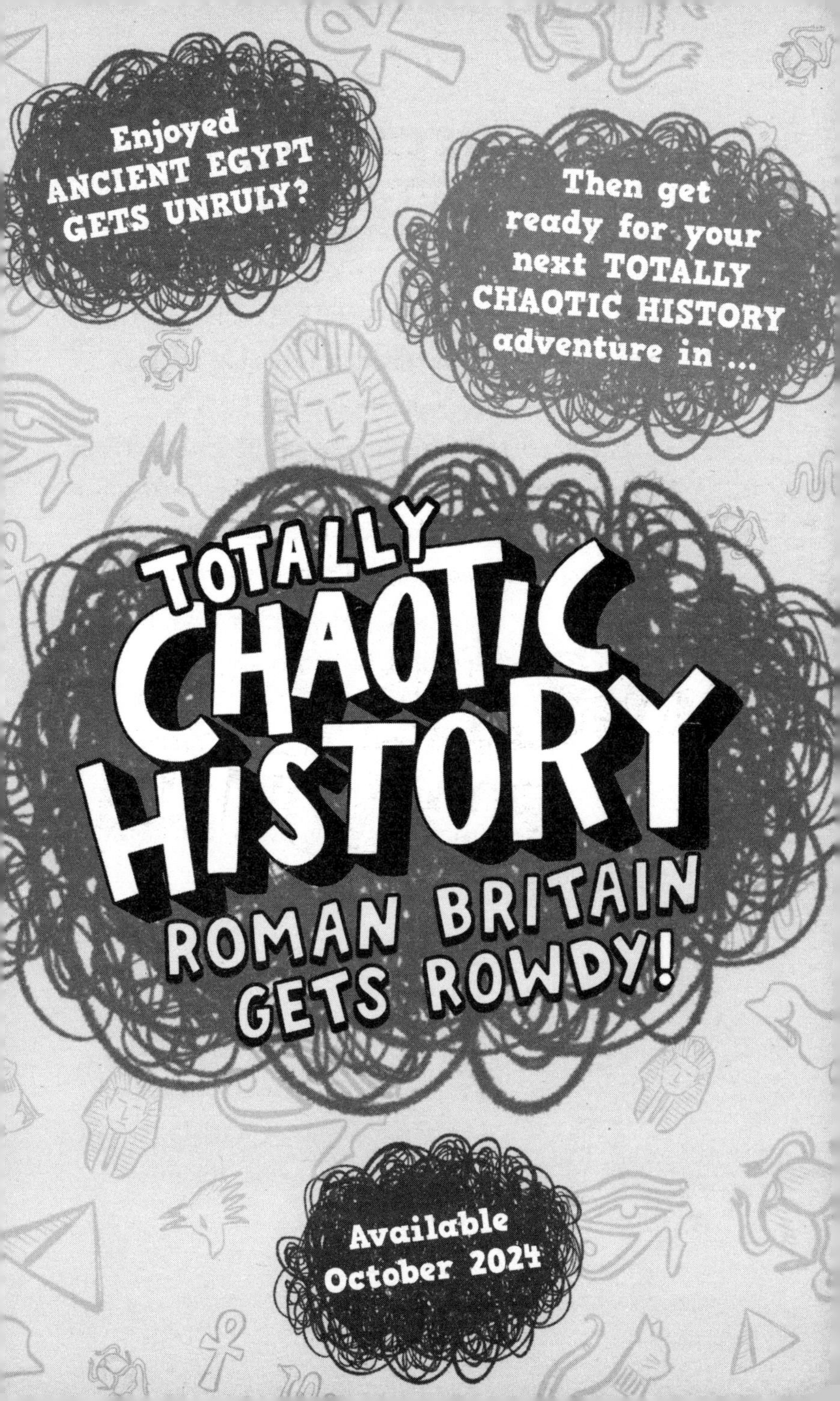

Enjoyed
ANCIENT EGYPT
GETS UNRULY?
Then get
ready for your
next TOTALLY
CHAOTIC HISTORY
adventure in ...
TOTALLY
CHAOTIC
HISTORY
ROMAN BRITAIN
GETS ROWDY!
Available
October 2024

MEET THE MAKERS

GREG JENNER is a public historian, author and broadcaster. He is best known for hosting the BBC's educational comedy podcasts *You're Dead to Me* and *Homeschool History*. As Historical Consultant to CBBC's BAFTA and Emmy award-winning TV comedy series "Horrible Histories", Greg was in charge of all the history facts for 1,500 side-splitting sketches and songs, and the spin-off movie. He has written three books for adults, and released his first children's book, *You Are History*, in 2022. Discover more at **gregjenner.com**

RIKIN PAREKH studied art at Camberwell College of Arts and the University of Westminster. When he's not drawing you'll probably find him at the cinema or at Comic Con. You can see more about Rikin at **rikinparekh.com**

MEET THE EGYPTOLOGIST

DR CAMPBELL PRICE is Curator of Egypt and Sudan at Manchester Museum, one of the UK's largest collections of Egyptian antiquities. He grew up in Glasgow and studied Egyptology at the University of Liverpool. You can find him online **@EgyptMcr**

I've been fascinated with the ancient Egyptians since I was six years old. My family took me to a museum, and I fell in love with the ancient Egyptian objects. Also my favourite cartoon baddie was a mummy! So much Egyptian stuff (monuments/ writings/belongings) is so well preserved, it seems to give us a window straight into their lives long ago – although we've got to be careful how we interpret things!